In Praise of the Impure

In Praise of the Impure

Poetry and the Ethical Imagination

Essays, 1980–1991

Alan Shapiro

TRIQUARTERLY BOOKS
NORTHWESTERN UNIVERSITY PRESS
Evanston, Illinois

TriQuarterly Books
Northwestern University Press
Evanston, Illinois 60208-4210

ISBN 0-8101-5025-5

Library of Congress Cataloging-in-Publication Data

Shapiro, Alan, 1952–
    In praise of the impure : poetry and the ethical imagination :
essays, 1980–1991 / Alan Shapiro.
        p.   cm.
    "TriQuarterly books."
    Includes bibliographical references (p.).
    ISBN 0-8101-5025-5 (alk. paper). — ISBN 0-8101-5028-X (pbk. :
alk. paper)
    1. American poetry—20th century—History and criticism.
2. Creative writing—Study and teaching. 3. Ethics in literature.
I. Title.
PS325.S48   1993
811'.509—dc20   93-30624
                                                             CIP

The paper used in this publication meets the minimum requirements of the American National
Standard for Information Sciences—Permanence of Paper for Printed Library Materials,
ANSI Z39.48-1984.

For Reg and Bob

Contents

Acknowledgments ix

Introduction...1

Part 1

The Flexible Rule: The Ethical Imagination 9

In Praise of the Impure: Narrative Consciousness in Poetry 30

Part 2

The New Formalism 61

Some Notes on Free Verse and Meter............................77

Part 3

"Far Lamps At Night": The Poetry of J. V. Cunningham...................93

Some Thoughts on Robert Hass 114

"Itinerary" by James McMichael.......................................121

The Liberal Imagination of Robert Pinsky's *Explanation of America*..127

"a living to fail": The Case of John Berryman 136

Part 4

The Dead Alive and Busy...153

Horace and the Reformation of Creative Writing............164

The Early Seventies and J. V. Cunningham....................182

Acknowledgments

I wish to thank especially Reginald Gibbons and Robert Von Hallberg for their criticism, encouragement, and friendship over the years. Without them, this book would not exist.

I am grateful to the following magazines and journals in which these essays or versions of them first appeared: *American Poetry Review*, "Horace and the Reformation of Creative Writing"; *Chicago Review*, "The Early Seventies and J. V. Cunningham" and "Some Thoughts on Robert Hass"; *Critical Inquiry*, "The New Formalism" and "Far Lamps At Night"; *Occident*, "'Itinerary' by James McMichael" and "The Liberal Imagination of Robert Pinsky's *Explanation of America*"; *TriQuarterly*, "The Flexible Rule," "In Praise of the Impure," "A Living To Fail," and "The Dead Alive and Busy."

I am also grateful to the following for permission to use extended quotations from copyrighted works.

John Berryman, from *The Dream Songs* (Farrar, Straus & Giroux, 1969). Copyright © 1959, 1962, 1963, 1964, 1965, 1966, 1967, 1968, 1969 by John Berryman. Reprinted by permission of the publisher.

Elizabeth Bishop, "The Moose," from *Complete Poems 1927–1979* (Farrar, Straus & Giroux, 1979). Copyright © 1976 by Elizabeth Bishop. Reprinted by permission of the publisher.

J. V. Cunningham, from *The Collected Poems and Epigrams of J. V. Cunningham* (Swallow Press, 1971). Copyright © 1971 by Ohio University Press. Reprinted by permission of the publisher.

Dana Gioia, "Cruising with the Beach Boys," from *Daily Horoscope* (Graywolf Press, Saint Paul, Minn., 1986). Copyright © 1986 by Dana Gioia. Reprinted by permission of the publisher.

Robert Hass, "Meditation at Lagunitas," from *Praise* (Ecco, 1979). Copyright © 1979 by Robert Hass. Reprinted by permission of the publisher.

Introduction

Though the essays in this book were written over an eleven-year period, individually they each subscribe to the same aesthetic, and collectively they represent the process by which that aesthetic was attained. The belief that animates my attention to poetry (and literary works in general) is that the formal and stylistic choices a writer makes are fraught with extraliterary judgments, biases, commitments that have moral as well as aesthetic implications. The Deep Image poet's aversion to complex syntactical arrangements in favor of simple sentences in which images and feelings float in loose association represents more than a literary preference. It is also, and more profoundly, the stylistic effect of an allegiance to the unconscious as the ultimate source of value, in life as well as art. Likewise, John Ashbery's devotion to the techniques of collage, argumentative cul de sacs, fractured narratives, bathos, and non sequiturs is the poetic equivalent of a view of life in which incomprehensible flux is continually disappointing our desire for meaning or coherence. Every way of writing, in other words, presupposes an implicit judgment about what's relevant or irrelevant in the rendering of a particular occasion; it tells us directly and indirectly not only what we ought to see but how we ought to see it. Even the formal principles within a poem, which govern the arrangement and selection of details, attitudes, and tones, are tacitly directing our attention to some aspects of experience, some possibilities of being, by dimming others. Style in the broadest sense, encompassing everything from rhythm to word choice, is consciousness in action. And it follows from this that some styles, some forms, can potentially enact a freer, more energetic play of consciousness than others. The literary and moral value or ideal that underlies these essays is inclusivity of mind and heart, the ability to be, in Henry James' terms, as "finely aware, [as] richly responsible," as possible.

Of course, inclusivity is a historically variable quality. It can manifest itself in any number of ways. And what may appear from one historical perspective as an exclusive procedure may seem from another as a necessary act of inclusion. Certain aspects of modernism, for instance, that appear now in retrospect to be primarily exclusive in nature—imagism's devotion to a language purified of discursiveness of any kind—had the salutary effect of making poetry more hos-

pitable to hitherto excluded areas of experience. All literary changes
are generated by the desire to get at what an established style or con-
vention overlooks, slights, or simplifies, to correct the overly artificial
with the sheer vitality of life or nature (romanticism), or the overly
animated with the disciplines of art (neoclassicism). But these
changes, in turn, produce conventions that inevitably simplify or out-
live the literary and historical conditions that made them necessary in
the first place, conventions which the following generation of writers
will likewise want to revise or overthrow in the name of extending
what the art can do. Which is just to say that all poems include some
things and exclude others. The only thoroughly inclusive poem is the
universe itself.

Eleven years ago when the earliest essay in this book was written, the
conventions which dominated the poetry scene derived primarily
from the experimental poets of the late fifties and sixties. The majority
of journals and periodicals across the country were filled with free
verse poems written in a flat, demotic style devoted primarily to the
presentation of surreal or quotidian images. Moreover, in the jour-
nals and magazines as well as in many books about contemporary
poetry, the defense of free verse experimentation and the disparage-
ment of metrical formality were built upon a number of false
dichotomies. Free verse was associated exclusively with liberated
feeling, spontaneity, fidelity to contemporary speech, and individual
expression, while meter was associated with intellectual control, or
calculation, emotional repression, and conformity to rules. The
polemical zeal of the oldest essays here arose in reaction to what
seemed to me back then and still seems now an uninformed antifor-
malism that pushed certain literary qualities—immediacy, suggestive-
ness, emotional intensity—to an unhealthy because exclusive
extreme. My quarrel then and now was not with the experimental
poetry of Rich, Wright, Bly, Kinnell, Lowell or Plath (to name only a
few of the important poets of that generation), so much as with the
invidious terms in which that poetry was praised, terms which the fol-
lowing generation of poets, my generation, accepted as sacred pieties
and used to justify a disabling ignorance of the prosodic past. That
older generation of poets began as formalists. And although most of
them abandoned meter and were better poets for doing so, the traces
of that formal training are still perceptible even in their most experi-
mental work. If nothing else, by learning how to write in form, they

were better able to solicit and fend off those formal echoes, so as to make their free verse rhythms more richly suggestive. In contrast, the lack of such formal training among many of the poets who began to publish in the mid to late seventies made much of their work seem utterly impoverished and uniform, despite the widespread belief that only free verse could liberate personal expression.

The situation today is very different. In the last several years, we have seen formal poetry come back into vogue. If free verse is still the dominant faith among most American poets, the new formalists have grown into a noisy sect of metrical dissenters. But this in turn has generated another set of problems. As I mention in "The New Formalism" and "Horace and the Reformation of Creative Writing," the new formalists' reaction to the poetic orthodoxies of the late seventies has perpetuated the same exclusive thinking in reverse, performing in effect an antinomian reversal of value: "good" now translates into metrical control, and evil into the irrationalities that free verse supposedly releases. The New Formalist exclusions, like the exclusions of the poetry against which it defines itself, have perpetuated a number of misconceptions about both meter and free verse, which I address in the two essays which comprise the second part of the book, "The New Formalism" and "Some Notes on Free Verse and Meter."

I have a greater appreciation of free verse now than I did eleven years ago, partly from reading more deeply the modern and postmodern poets who have mastered a variety of free verse lines, and partly from the free verse I myself have written. The distinction between free and formal verse is finally less important than the necessity to keep whatever form one chooses keenly responsive to the occasion it articulates. When metrical conventions of any kind fail to enhance the acts of attention they're attempting to perform, when they dissociate themselves from content, they lose moral and emotional substance; yet when properly deployed to yield the rhythmical effect of fine awareness, they are indispensable to the creative exploration of emotional and moral worlds.

The book is organized in four sections. The first, comprising "The Flexible Rule" and "In Praise of the Impure," lays out in general terms the aesthetic and moral principles that inform all the other essays in the book. These are more recent essays. They represent, in effect, the theoretical results to which the other essays in the book have brought me. The issues that these essays investigate—the need for, and limitation of, formulaic rules in making sense of the concrete particulars of lived experience, the ways in which specific situations condition the application of general principles in aesthetic, moral, and legal contexts—are then explored in the essays of part 2 ("The New Formalism" and "Some Notes On Free Verse and Meter") in the more technical context of poetic form. The imagination that explores in the ethical realm the tension between concrete situations and general rules is the same imagination that aspires to achieve in the handling of form an expressive tension between repetition and surprise, the familiar and the strange, the expected and the unforeseen.

The salient feature of imagination is to bring together what our conventions tell us should be kept apart. Imagination is the something within us "that doesn't love a wall," that seeks to violate boundaries, transgress borders, challenge our customary ways of thinking and feeling so as to make our rules, systems, habitual perceptions more responsive to a wider range of life. It is the life-redeeming agent of impurity, and it stands implacably opposed to the equally powerful human impulse for the pure, the unambiguous, the perfectly controlled. The poets I write about in part 3 embody in varying degrees both impulses. This section, I should add, is not intended as a survey of the best and worst aspects of American poetry in the postwar period (though I think Pinsky, McMichael, and Cunningham are all important poets, and Cunningham especially has never received the recognition he deserves). These rather are some of the poets who despite the differences between them led me to the view of imagination, poetic form, and the dangers of exclusive thinking which the other essays articulate more directly.

Let me also add that my judgment about particular poems has changed since the writing of some of these essays. For instance, when I wrote the piece on James McMichael, his *Four Good Things* had not yet been published in its entirety, and the comments I make about it were based on an excerpt that appeared under the title "The McMichaels," in the Carcanet anthology *Five American Poets*. Once the poem was published in book form, and I had had the opportunity to live with it for several years, I was able to perceive and appreciate the extraordinary power of the poem's meditative sweep, its ability to connect public and private experience in convincing and illuminating ways, and its subtle measure that simultaneously seems like poetry on the verge of speech, and speech on the verge of poetry. I still regard "Itinerary" as one of the best American poems ever written.

Robert Pinksy's more recent work, *History of My Heart* and *The Want Bone*, has only confirmed my judgment that he's one of our most daring and experimental poets. Though in these last two books he has greatly modified his style, becoming much less essayistic and discursive than in his first two books, *Sadness and Happiness* and *An Explanation of America*, his method is still essentially jazz-like improvisation. He now does primarily though not exclusively with images, concrete particulars, myths and dreams, what he once did primarily though not exclusively with ideas. The structure of his poems may be more alogical and fragmentary, his diction more compressed and figurative, but the same brisk, inquisitive, richly expressive syntax still fuels the movement of his verse, enabling him to cover so much ground so economically. From poem to poem, book to book, Pinsky has reinvented himself not by abandoning anything he's learned along the way but by adding to it. He's refined his art without diminishing what the art can do. This is what I've found especially instructive in the evolution of his work.

Since most American poets now teach in the university, it seems appropriate to conclude this book with a few essays on the related issues of the teaching of poetry, the education of the poet, and the effect of the university environment on the contemporary practice of the art. In recent years, many critics in and out of academia have blamed the rise of creative writing programs for the decline of American poetry from an art with broad cultural appeal to a specialized activity confined to the closed world of the classroom. Poetry, these critics tell us, is read only by other poets, all of whom either teach or study in the writing programs. That institutional pressures have shaped the practice of poetry since it moved into the university is certainly true. On the other hand, to claim that writing programs alone are responsible for the formation of what one writer calls a university-supported subculture insulated from a general nonspecialist audience is to mistake effects for causes. It may tell us something about why no one outside the university is reading *contemporary* poetry, but it tells us nothing about why few people outside the university are reading poetry at all. In "Horace and the Reformation of Creative Writing," I explore some of the cultural and historical reasons for this phenomenon, and I also devote a portion of the essay to examining the ways in which creative writing is currently taught and to considering how our writing programs might better serve their mission of educating writers.

Finally let me say that this is not an impartial, comprehensive, or especially generous book on contemporary poetry. Criticism by a poet is always, directly or indirectly, attempting to create a favorable climate for the poetry he or she has written, is writing, or desires to write. Though I haven't arranged these essays chronologically, the order in which they were written traces my artistic as well as critical development. All of them were motivated by the need to make the strongest possible case for the poets I admire, poets on whom my own work is or has been modeled, whose poems, "finely aware [and] richly responsible," make artistic strength impossible to tell from moral excellence.

1992

Part 1

The Flexible Rule:
The Ethical Imagination

This is a book about the ethical imagination, specifically about the way in which poetry and fiction can enact a kind of ethical play, testing and revising our moral certitudes through a vigilant appeal to the complexities of circumstance. By *ethical* play I mean an activity of consciousness concerned with ethical problems as they occur in lived experience, embedded in the densely tangled web of contingent happenings, commitments, practical realities, values, needs, and desires which constitute our individual and collective lives. By ethical *play* I mean an activity of consciousness which tries to turn what we are used to, what is most familiar and therefore most difficult to know, into an ethical problem which we then attempt to solve. Thus ethical play involves a kind of paradoxical habit of mind—a tolerance for ambiguity, for the shifting and indeterminate on the one hand, and a hunger for clarity on the other. For if we come to experience inescapably freighted with principles and values which help us negotiate and organize the world, the world in turn is larger, messier and more resistant than our conceptual schemes imply. It is one thing to believe in the Ten Commandments as a moral guide, but quite another and more difficult thing to follow them, given the mutable conditions within which we have to live. The moral imperatives we try to live by may reduce and help control the unpredictable, but they can never entirely eliminate it. And it follows from this that the strength of an ethical system may reside as much in its ability to accommodate the contingencies of particular and unanticipated situations as in its bedrock, nonnegotiable values. The practical reasoning of ethics, then, requires more than the mechanical application of a set of rules; like "poetic reasoning" it entails attention to particulars, a readiness for the surprising, and some capacity to improvise. The general who sticks to his battle plan after the enemy has discovered how to subvert it, instead of adjusting to a different strategy, will be soundly defeated. The neuropsychologist encountering some hitherto unknown mental disorder would be less than effective if the treatment he devises were to adhere exclusively to the norms of current practice. (See A. R. Luria's *The Man with a Shattered World: The History of a Brain Wound*, Harvard University Press, 1987). The writer, too, who's not alive to the possibilities of circumstance but simplifies experience to fit a predetermined plan gives up in fullness and complexity of vision what he or she may gain in the clarity of narrow focus.

The English jurist H. L. A. Hart maintains that all moral and legal systems consist of "a core of settled meanings and a penumbral area where their application to a set of facts is debatable, and where no judgment in either direction could in any absolute way be demonstrated to be wrong and right." What I want to argue is that the imaginative thinking expressed in certain kinds of stories or poems occupies this shadowy area between particulars and generalities, rules and exceptions. And just as a judge should attempt to pay full and sensitive attention to the facts and principles involved in deciding a particular case, considering the widest range of implications and consequences of this or that course of action, so also the imagination, in occupying that penumbral area, tries to remind us of what our various programs suppress, what our picture of the world excludes, how our various clarities—necessary as they are—always entail some sort of cost, some sort of blindness.

Poetry attempts to train us not to suspend our judgments (for we live by judging, choosing to do this rather than that) but how to judge better by keeping our judgments flexibly responsive to the widest range of possibility. In *The Fragility of Goodness: Luck and Ethics in Greek Tragedy and Philosophy* (Cambridge University Press, 1986), Martha Nussbaum summarizes Aristotle's nonscientific conception of choice in similar terms: "Aristotle tells us that a person who attempts to make every decision by appeal to some antecedent general principle held firm and inflexible for the occasion is like an architect who tries to use a straight ruler on the intricate curves of a fluted column. Instead, the good architect will, like the builders of Lesbos, measure with a flexible strip of metal that 'bends round to fit the shape of the stone and is not fixed.'" The ethical imagination is like this supple ruler, bending round to fit the shape of each experience, keeping our certitudes attentive to that penumbral area where judgment stands in tension with sympathy, and principle with circumstance, bringing our certitudes to bear upon the most compelling and difficult occasions so as to test their limits and resiliencies.

This conception of the ethical imagination entails several presuppositions. It presupposes the existence of certain kinds of objective truths, at least as they are understood, ratified, and described by a particular culture; and also that these truths are accessible by means only of a flexible kind of attention to details, or appraisal of specific contexts. This appraisal, moreover, can be performed only by individual agents. Of course, as individuals we operate within discursive worlds replete with various conventions, conventions which set constraints upon what we can think or know. Within those constraints, however, by virtue of the particulars of temperament, training, circumstance, and that empathetic power of entering into the moral experience of others, we have a capacity for ethical discrimination. And this capacity, in turn, can alter the very conventions which inform it. That is, I conceive of ethical appraisal as a continual dialectic in which this power of mind is shaped by and is always shaping the conventions within which it is performed. Now, I ascribe a similar sort of agency to authors. This means that within and through literary conventions (and also, as we will see, moral and legal ones) they can depict in their work both acts of moral appraisal and the contexts within which those acts take place. Here, however, two qualifications are necessary. One is that this description of writers is appropriate only to writing of an essentially realist kind. The other is that this general picture is radically at variance with, on the one hand, some current theories (structuralist/poststructuralist/Marxist) which emphasize the sociolinguistic construction of and constraints upon our individual lives and deny the kind of empathetic, creative, and volitional independence I am ascribing to them; and, on the other, with the cult of "openness" which dominates the practice and teaching of creative writing. While a majority of literary theorists adhere to some deterministic system which narrows the possibilities of choice and judgment within specific situations, most poets and teachers of poetry think that empathy and negative capability can substitute for judgment altogether.

Certainly, as George Eliot reminds us, judgment—at least as it appears in art—"is always false unless it is checked and enlightened by perpetual reference to the special circumstances that mark the individual fate." And this requires some sort of sympathetic reach or heightened receptivity, some capacity to step outside our assumptions and predilections and enter into other lives so as to make them accessible to our understanding. To understand the experience of others may presuppose some initial act of sympathy. But if all we do is pass chameleonlike into another life, we leave ourselves no basis for determining the significance of the experience we seek to understand. That is, to understand experience means in some sense to place it in relation to our needs and values, to see what it is good for. Sympathy divorced from judgment is as incomplete, as false, as judgment which stands too magisterially over and against the special circumstances of the individual. Moreover, though we like to think that Keatsian empathy is itself a moral property, it seems to me more true to say it's a morally neutral quality of mind that can have moral consequences, but in and of itself implies no moral position or principle, since uninformed by some particular judgment it can take morally contradictory forms. Thus, by upbringing and temperament someone could be predisposed to feel especially sympathetic to the plight of Nazis after Hitler; or to the criminally insane; to striking coal miners or to the bosses they strike against. Or my negative capability may be so acute and indiscriminate that I sympathize with everyone, good and bad alike, and am unable thus to weigh the justness of competing claims. Think in this connection of the souls we meet in the third canto of Dante's *Inferno*. These are the living dead who, Virgil tells us, lived without praise or blame and are therefore relegated only to the outskirts of hell, spurned by the damned as well as by the blessed. Their sin was moral neutrality. And whether this arose from too much or too little empathy, equal concern for everyone or equal indifference, either extreme amounts to the same ethical paralysis. Exiled from heaven and hell alike, they share this moral no-man's-land with those angels who neither rebelled with Satan nor kept faith with God but merely stood apart, in sympathy perhaps for both opposing points of view.

The imagination mediates between the moral and sympathetic faculties, between that which separates so as to discern and order, and that which merges so as to feel, participating in both, restricted to neither, encouraging flexibility of response when our responses grow straightedged and rigid, and firmness of measure when they're ill-defined and too pliantly at the mercy of occasion.

2

If literature is, in Kenneth Burke's suggestive phrase, "equipment for living," living, in turn, is the necessary equipment for literature. It's possible to understand a poem or story superficially, in isolation from the world that generates it. To read more profoundly, though, to realize its meaning with our very nerves, is quite another matter. This requires a kind of readiness which only life itself can give us. This is what Eugenio Montale means when he talks about the second life of poetry, the life it takes on in us years after our initial reading, when it coalesces with some unforeseen experience, when some occasion suddenly recalls it, and it comes to us bearing its gift of revelation. The process is of course reciprocal, for reading itself is part of life, and literature prepares us for the reception of experience just as much and continually as experience prepares us for the reception, the realization, of a story or poem.

Very powerfully ten years ago I discovered this second life of literature in connection with Herman Melville's novel *Billy Budd*. I first read *Billy Budd* in high school or college, at an age and in a context where it could mean little more to me than an academic exercise. In 1978, though, when I was living in the San Francisco area, the extraordinary trial of Dan White sent me back to it. For both the novel—particularly the trial scene which stands at the center of it—and the Dan White case brought into painful focus the knotty, complex issues of sympathy and judgment which moral and literary acts entail. Comparing the two, moreover, helped me to see and understand the salient features of both trials, features I would not have seen so clearly had I encountered either trial in isolation.

Dan White, you'll recall, was the San Francisco city supervisor who murdered Mayor George Moscone and Harvey Milk, a fellow supervisor and gay-rights activist. White's attorney mounted what came to be called the "Twinkies Defense," pleading for a verdict of voluntary manslaughter on the grounds of temporary insanity (the technical term for this is "diminished capacity") brought on by two Twinkies White had eaten on the morning of the crime, thus turning him homicidal by raising the level of sugar in his blood and violently intensifying a manic-depressive tendency. As a good defense attorney will do, White's lawyer appealed throughout the trial to the jurors' biases; all of them were, like White himself, working-class people disaffected with a liberal city government they regarded as more responsive to the morally aberrant and socially marginal than to themselves, the mainstream, law-abiding citizenry. Indeed, White himself was elected to office on a staunchly conservative platform of law and order. As he wrote in his campaign literature, "I am not going to be forced out of San Francisco by splinter groups of radicals, social deviates, and incorrigibles. You must realize there are thousands upon thousands of frustrated angry people such as yourselves waiting to unleash a fury that can and will eradicate the malignancies which blight our beautiful city." He represented the interests of those who believed in the received, if ill-defined, conventional values of family, country, and God. And throughout his term in office he was continually opposed and frustrated by what he perceived to be the double-dealing and corruption of city politics. Time and again he was outmaneuvered by the more politically adroit and more flamboyant Harvey Milk, whose progressive policies and homosexuality came to embody everything that White opposed. Partly because of these frustrations, and partly because of the financial strains of trying to raise a family on a city supervisor's meager salary (his wife had just recently given birth to their first child), White resigned his seat. Ten days later, in response to pressure from the Police Association and the Board of Realtors, whose interests Dan White also represented, he asked Moscone for his seat back, and Moscone at first agreed, and then because of pressure from the gay community, particularly from Harvey Milk, he reneged on his promise and appointed someone more politically congenial to the board of supervisors. To White, the decorated Vietnam vet, the ex-cop, ex-fireman, hardworking family man, this seemed like the ultimate betrayal, and the rage it triggered, a rage compounded by the myriad other pressures he was under at the time, and apparently by the junk food he ate that morning for breakfast, pushed him over the edge of sanity and made him strike back at the two men he thought responsible for his political demise.

Ideally, in a court of law evidence and not emotion is supposed to rule. Not that emotion can ever be eliminated in the adjudication of a case. But what the evidentiary rules try to ensure is that the biases in favor of or against a defendant be minimized as much as possible so that the evidence itself determines judgment. Which is to say, a jury is only as reasonable as the evidence that's brought before it. And without question the defense made a more effective argument than the prosecution, which throughout the trial seemed disorganized, unprepared and halfhearted in pursuing a conviction of first-degree murder. Aside from the fact that Tom Norman, the prosecuting attorney, took only three days to present his case and seldom cross-examined the array of psychiatrists, social workers, friends, and relatives whom the defense called to testify for White, he never himself raised the question of motive, never so much as alluded to the political feuding between White and Moscone, and White and Milk. Instead, as Randy Shilts points out in his biography of Harvey Milk, *The Mayor of Castro Street* (St. Martin's, 1988), "Norman had simply given the chronology of the murders without a hint of the motive." (Motive, of course—"malice aforethought"—is one of the crucial elements in the legal definition of first-degree murder.) Moreover, during the jury selection process, Norman used only six of his twenty-six preemptory challenges and thereby allowed the defense to pack the jury with white working-class ethnic Catholics, like White himself. Whatever the reasons, and conspiracy theories abounded at the time, the prosecution never contested the defense's central thesis that "good people, fine people, with fine backgrounds"—people like the jurors themselves—"simply don't kill people in cold blood."

As my brief summary indicates, the story the defense attorney told was tailored to fit the biases and fears of the jury. It's a story which emphasized Dan White's background and character; it appealed to the jurors' sympathies, their identification with a man who was presented to them as no more a murderer than they were, a man who shared their values, their concern for family, but whose high ideals were poorly suited for the slick practicalities city politics required. "Dan White," the defense attorney argued, "was supremely frustrated with crime and the politics of the city, and saw the city deteriorating as a place for the average and decent people to live." The city government itself and its liberal policies were put on trial, while Dan White and the beleaguered values he represented were portrayed as victims, a portrayal the prosecution never challenged. The jury from the start was predisposed in White's favor, so much so that even when the prosecution played the tape of White's confession taken hours after the crime, four of the jurors were brought to tears by his tortured voice describing the various pressures that finally made him snap. It was no surprise then that the jury found Dan

White guilty of just two counts of voluntary manslaughter, for which White was sentenced to seven years of prison.

Beyond determining whether or not a defendant has committed an alleged offense (in Dan White's case there was no ambiguity on this point), a court of law does more than merely fit a legal statute to a particular act. Insofar as it also allows social and psychological contingencies to inform how a legal statute should apply to that act, the judicial process bears important similarities to the ethical imagination, as I described it earlier. In a sense, the interplay of argument and counterargument, sympathetic or unsympathetic appeal and counterappeal, which the defense and prosecution bring before a jury, is the judicial equivalent of the imaginative play literary works enact. A writer tries to exercise the fullest range of faculties upon his subject so that whatever judgment is attained emerges from a full engagement with the experiential evidence. He fails, moreover, when he tries to force the evidence to fit a preconceived idea, when his judgment seems a measure of his insulation from experience, not engagement with it. Likewise, the judicial process ideally tries to bring the fullest play of argument before a jury, and it follows from this that the more vigorous the play, the greater chance there'll be for a fair and responsible hearing. Where there's collusion, however, or incompetence, no serious play occurs. In the Dan White trial, only a semblance of this interplay took place, and consequently only one argument was heard, an argument which shaped the evidence so as to appeal to the feelings and values of a conservative, homophobic jury who identified with White, and for whom White became a kind of lightning rod for their own sense of fear, anger, and powerlessness.

Their sympathetic judgment, though, triggered a riot of sterner judgments in the streets. Hours after the verdict was handed down, thousands of gays gathered at City Hall. Chanting slogans like "Dan White, Dan White/Hit man for the New Right" and "All straight jury/no surprise/Dan White lives/And Harvey dies," they rioted through the night, breaking windows, torching police cars and battling the police. Randy Shilts reports that as a young man torched a last police car, he shouted to a reporter, "Make sure you put in the paper that I ate too many Twinkies."

3

The trial Melville depicts represents to my mind an equally extreme but diametrically opposed response to the tension between judgment and sympathy. For if the jurors in the Dan White case seemed to consider only the extenuating circumstances of the crime, Captain Vere, in judging Billy, considers only the crime itself, the violated rule of law, and none of the mitigating factors, including the love he feels for the man he must condemn.

This story is simpler in outline than the Dan White case yet it dramatizes a more complicated set of problems. Serving on a British warship in the last decade of the eighteenth century, in the revolutionary era, Billy Budd, an impressed sailor, is called before the captain and falsely accused of conspiracy by John Claggart, the master of arms, a man of innate depravity, bent on destroying Billy for no reason beyond the fact that Billy has an innocent heart, good looks, and is liked by everyone. Being unreflective and, when agitated, incapable of speech, Billy responds to the accusation by striking and killing Claggart. The trial that follows brings into dramatic focus a host of oppositions which the story up to this point has raised. The most obvious one, of course, is that embodied in Billy and Claggart— an opposition not just between good and evil but between two innate and "natural" propensities, one of which stands outside the trappings of civilized life and is ill-suited to the "moral obliquities" and "sinister dexterities" that civilized life requires, and the other which easily "folds itself into the mantle of respectability," manipulating all of the external qualities we think of as pertaining to the preservation of a rational life—sobriety, deference, self-control—so as to satisfy an irrational aim. Whereas Billy is described as an "upright barbarian" with a nature as simple and innocent as "Adam before the urbane serpent wriggled himself into his company," Claggart's nature "has no vulgar alloy of the brute" in it, but is dominated by intellectuality, and "a cool judgment sagacious and sound." Feeling and reason, "primeval nature" and "formalized humanity," the claims of private conscience versus the expediencies of public order—these are some of the antitheses which the characters of Budd and Claggart evoke, and which Captain Vere internalizes during the trial scene.

Captain Vere occupies a kind of psychological middle ground between the extremes Billy and Claggart symbolize. He comprehends and is deeply moved by Billy's essential innocence but because of his

position of authority is compelled to act strictly in accordance with
the military code of law. He strongly feels the claims of private con-
science but must act against them. To treat such a capital offense with
any leniency, especially in time of war and shortly after the Nore and
Spithead mutinies, would set a dangerous example for the other
sailors. Thus, he insists to his uncertain and wavering officers that
they exclude from their judgment all questions of provocation and
motive, which is a matter "for psychologic theologians to discuss. But
what has a military court to do with it? . . . The prisoner's deed—with
that alone we have to do." The emotional considerations to which the
jurors in the Dan White case succumbed, Vere excludes without at the
same time denying the force, emotional and moral, of such considera-
tions. His very movements during the trial dramatize his sense of con-
flict: "Turning, he to-and-fro paced the cabin athwart; in the return-
ing ascent to windward climbing the slant deck in the ship's lee roll,
without knowing it symbolizing thus in his action a mind resolute to
surmount difficulties even if against primitive instincts strong as the
wind and the sea." We see in Vere the effects of war upon the ethical
imagination. For if it is imagination which enables Vere to see and feel
beyond his military role, to perceive within this situation the moral
ambiguities and injustices which the military law cannot acknowl-
edge, the exigencies of war, in turn, prohibit him from acting in accor-
dance with those feelings and perceptions. Wars, even just wars,
thrive on the narrowing of moral agency, reducing the self as much as
possible to a military instrument whose efficiency depends on limiting
free deliberation and flexibility of thought and feeling, capacities
which the ethical imagination tries to cultivate. Thus, when Billy
cries out, just before his execution, "God bless Captain Vere!" Vere
shows no emotion, but stands "rigid as a musket in the shiparmorer's
rack."

Yet if we're encouraged, as I think we are, to sympathize with
Vere, our sympathy isn't meant to be unqualified. True, Melville does
go to great lengths to describe the context which influences Vere's
decision: considering the revolutionary temper of the times and the
recent mutinies which beset the British navy, some of whose partici-
pants are currently on board his ship, plus the particular scouting
expedition he is undertaking, not to mention the fact that when the
murder happens the *Bellipotent* is farthest from the fleet, Vere could
hardly have acted differently. At the same time, the depiction of
Vere's character isn't unambiguous. Though the narrator tells us

Vere has "a marked leaning toward everything intellectual," and that he loves books, particularly those "treating of actual men and events no matter of what era—history, biography, and unconventional writers like Montaigne, who, free from cant and convention, honestly and in the spirit of common sense philosophize upon realities"—we also learn that Vere is a man of fixed ideas and settled principles, someone for whom reading does not change or enlarge his mind but only confirms "his own more reserved thoughts": " . . . there had got to be established in him some positive convictions which he forefelt would abide in him essentially unmodified so long as his intelligent part remained unimpaired," convictions, the narrator goes on to say, which "were as a dike against those invading waters of novel opinion social, political and otherwise, which carried away as in a torrent no few minds in those days. . . . " We sympathize with Vere's dilemma; at the same time we see his limitations, that he seems too readily disposed by temperament and character to resolve any moral ambiguities through the austere application of rule, even if this is what the necessities of war require. What makes Vere so interesting is that in terms of feeling and perception he is like the good architect whose supple measure can "bend round to fit the shape of the occasion," but in terms of judgment he is like the one whose rule is straightedged, even on a fluted column.

The character, though, who most approximates the Aristotelian ideal of a flexibly inclusive vision is the narrator of the tale. It is the narrator who, directly or indirectly, reminds us continually of the most profound dichotomy which underlies the others we have mentioned, the dichotomy between the closure of the "measured forms" we live by and the radical complexity of truth, irreducibly ambiguous and many-sided and which our rules and systems attempt to tidy up in order to control. This dichotomy is crucially involved with the problem of representation, for, as the narrator tells us, "The symmetry of form attainable in pure fiction cannot so readily be achieved in a narration essentially having less to do with fable than with fact. Truth uncompromisingly told will always have its ragged edges." Throughout the novel, moreover, the narrator distinguishes between the story he's attempting to relate—a story which aims at the fullness of truth and is therefore, in its fidelity to detail, necessarily digressive and loosely shaped, and whose judgments and sympathies are complex and guarded—and those narrations which simplify in order to serve ulterior purposes and interests, like the naval historians who may

make mention of mutinies without supplying the politically unflatter-
ing details, or like the published, official version of the murder and
execution which we are given at the novel's end, which reshapes the
events and characters (Billy as foreign-born criminal and Claggart as
English victim) so as to reinforce the ideals of war and discipline. The
narrator likewise distinguishes the aim and method of his own narra-
tion from other literary genres—from the patriotic songs of Dibdin,
for instance, which serve as "no mean auxiliary to the English gov-
ernment," and from the Gothic romance which has to do primarily
with mysteries of plot, and not (as his tale does) with mysteries of
character, which don't permit of any easy resolution. The novel's
dramatizing, complex, open form represents Melville's allegiance to
the ethical imagination and its preoccupation with penumbral areas,
zones of experience which are inherently problematic and where no
absolute judgment of right or wrong is available.

The narrator, of course, is not participating in the events which
he describes and can therefore afford a luxury of vision not available
to the characters themselves. Yet what the narrator's fidelity to the
truth with all its jagged edges helps us see is how "'the forms, mea-
sured forms'" which Vere confides in are as morally unstable and lim-
iting as they are socially necessary. In putting Billy to death, Vere
upholds and safeguards the public order not just to serve the purpos-
es of war, but also—so we learn later—to satisfy "the most secret of all
passions, ambition, never attained to the fulness of fame," because he
dies in battle shortly after Billy's execution. And if Vere is the
upholder of forms, Claggart, the master of arms, is the master of
forms, manipulating public order to carry out a private hate.

And this in turn raises another question. If we measure the
sophistication of a legal system not just by its laws but by the flexibil-
ity with which the laws are fitted to particular occasions, by their elas-
ticity in relation to penumbral areas, we must acknowledge that this
pliancy is also what provides a refuge for the sort of evil Claggart dra-
matizes. It allows evil an orderly continuance; it allows, too, for the
distorting appeals to sympathetic feeling which that other master of
forms, the lawyer for Dan White, was able to achieve. Melville's own
political allegiance may fall closer to the humane yet conservative
Vere than to the "bloody reforms" going on across the channel. As a
citizen, he may believe with Montaigne, Vere's favorite author, that
"the greatness of mind is not so much to draw up and hale forward, as
to know how to range, direct, and circumscribe itself." As an artist,

though, whose ultimate allegiance is to the truth and all its jagged edges, he sees that custom, to quote Montaigne again, "is a violent and deceiving school-mistress," that "nothing can be certainly established," both the judging and the judged being in continual alteration and motion, and that we should not be "servilely subjected to common laws, but rather with judgment and voluntary liberty apply ourselves unto them."

4

The world of the *Agamemnon*, the first play in Aeschylus' *Oresteia*, is sunk in various conflicting darknesses, and what light there is is only the false light of murderous self-justification which further deepens and perpetuates the violent gloom. This is a world fraught with pious killers, all appealing to a different history to justify their crimes—a world in which moral claim clashes with moral claim, in which allegiance to one good violates another, and not just between the principal characters but also, and more poignantly, within their minds and hearts. What the play examines is not so much how the characters act, since all the actions are predetermined and inescapable, but how they respond, emotionally and psychologically, to the dilemma they inherit, how they attempt to simplify the moral complexity that faces them in order to act the way they do.

Agamemnon is our case in point. "The jugglery of circumstance" has placed him, as it does Vere, between two bad alternatives, two mutually exclusive claims. To appease Artemis and carry out the expedition against Troy, he has to sacrifice his daughter, Iphigenia, but in so doing he will incur the anger of the earth gods, the ancient protectors of the hearth, of familial ties and obligations. Or he can sacrifice the Trojan expedition and save his daughter but in so doing offend almighty Zeus. Either way he risks impiety. "My fate is angry if I disobey these, but angry if I slaughter this child, the beauty of my house, with maiden bloodshed staining these father's altars." Once he decides to sacrifice Iphigenia, though, something peculiar happens. His emotional turmoil disappears. "It is right," he says. "May all be right in the end." In her discussion of the play, Martha Nussbaum shows us how Agamemnon "from the moment he makes his decision itself, the best he could have made . . . strangely turns himself into a collaborator, a willing victim." For Vere, the inner agony, the emotional dilemma, continues and intensifies, even after he decides which course of action he must take. At the moment of decision the "military disciplinarian" replaces the father in him without at the same time destroying it. He continues to feel the full force of the conflicting claims, the full range of its emotional implications. For Agamemnon, as Nussbaum demonstrates, the command to sacrifice his daughter enables him to sacrifice his fatherly attachment. Ignoring her "pitying looks," he has her lifted, so the Chorus tells us, "as you might lift a goat for sacrifice." Nussbaum observes that "his only acknowledgment of her human status is his command to stop her mouth, so she will not utter inauspicious curses against his house. And even this command uses animal language: they are to check her voice 'by the force and the voiceless power of the bridle.'" One can see the psychological utility of such coldheartedness; it insulates him from the full effects of what he's doing; it releases him from conflict. But it thereby diminishes him as a human being. Thus the chorus tells us how "from the heart the breath came bitter and sacrilegious, utterly infidel, to warp a will now to be stopped at nothing." Though the killing has the sanction of divine command, it is as if, under the cover of that sanction, Agamemnon gives in to an unholy and violent passion, as if the killing's unavoidable necessity enables him to act out a forbidden bestiality, a bestiality that desecrates the familial order.

As Clytaemnestra says, to justify her murderous act of vengeance "with no thought more than if a beast had died . . . he slaughtered like a victim his own child." And yet like Agamemnon she simplifies her vision of her situation, for she too is caught between conflicting ties, and can neither act nor refuse to act without incurring blame. Thus she absolutizes one claim—she is Iphigenia's mother—and denies the other (as she tells the chorus, "speak of me never more as the wife of Agamemnon"), so as to kill her husband without remorse, with a kind of blasphemous delight: "When he was down I struck him the third blow, in thanks to Zeus the lord of dead men underneath the ground . . . and as he died he spattered me with the dark red and violent driven rain of bitter savored blood to make me glad, as gardens stand among the showers of God in glory at the birthtime of the buds."

What we have here are two rival conceptions of justice, one associated with the feminine, private world of home and family loyalties and one associated with the public, male-dominated world of war and civic enterprise, which feeds off the children mothers rear. These antithetical allegiances, moreover, mediate almost everything each character says or sees. The allegiances circumscribe the characters' vision and the range of their responsiveness. Clytaemnestra, for instance, thinks exclusively in terms of family relations. Even her description of the murder is fraught, ironically, with images of fertility and nurturance (blood falling like rain over gardens "at the birth-time of the buds"). Likewise, when she describes the taking of Troy, she's compelled to depict not Achaean glory, but the familial devastation which the Trojans themselves have suffered ("children lean to clasp the aged who begot them, crying upon the death of those most dear, from lips that never will be free"); she doesn't revel in victory but warns against the excesses victory can license ("Oh, let there be no fresh wrong done!"). Agamemnon's account of the same event says nothing at all about the family. He dissolves the concrete human realities of loss and pain into a generalized metaphor of "a wild and bloody lion" swarming "above the towers of Troy to gut its hunger lapping at the blood of kings." Inhabiting a world of citizens and soldiers, not husbands and brothers, he thinks strictly in terms of conquest and public glory. Thus, his first concern upon returning home is "the business of the city." The bloody lion becomes the public doctor who "must use medicine, or burn, or amputate" to remove the civic corruption which has flared up in his absence. That anything could be amiss at home does not occur to him.

Only the chorus seems to move between these rival worlds of value, acknowledging the justness and necessity of each without restricting their sympathies or judgments to either. They understand, as Agamemnon and Clytaemnestra can't, that our human status is a middle state between the sky gods and the gods of earth, and that the powers of both—in their terms, of reason and instinct, light and dark, male and female, choice and necessity—comprise our very being. They also understand that this heterogeneous condition is dangerous, that our mixed allegiances can lead to conflict, and that conflict in turn can tempt us to simplify or purify our lives in one direction or the other. Like the narrator of *Billy Budd*, their allegiance is to the truth and all its jagged edges, and they therefore represent the ethical imagination in action, making themselves throughout the play, as Nussbaum puts it, "look, notice, respond, and remember, cultivating responsiveness by working through the memory of these events, until 'the painful memory of pain drips, instead of sleep, before the heart.'" What they demand of the antagonists, and where they hold them accountable, is in their emotional and imaginative responses to the crimes they commit. Against the psychological evasions of an Agamemnon, which help suppress the painful moral consequences of his actions, the old men of the chorus remind us that "wisdom comes alone through suffering." Only by responding fully to experience, with feeling as well as intellect can we achieve an understanding adequate to the complexities we face. Had Agamemnon done so, he might have realized through the grief he felt the depth of his attachment to his daughter. He might have apprehended more clearly than he does the value of that attachment and the familial consequences sacrificing it would bring. In continuing to feel the force of both competing claims, even after he commits himself to one of them, he might have understood more poignantly the cost of political commitment, the personal and moral cost of war, and might have made himself a more judicious, more attentive ruler. And upon returning home he might have been a better husband, sensitive to Clytaemnestra, or if not sensitive at least aware that things at home, within his household, could not be as he had left them ten years earlier.

If Clytaemnestra and Agamemnon seem impervious to remorse, if they avoid the full emotional consequences of their actions and thereby act without learning (in contrast to the chorus, who learn but never act), there is at least a kind of moral progress for their son, Orestes, who seems closer to the choral ideal of full responsiveness. Though his first reaction to killing his mother is to call her "some water snake, some viper," he also grieves "for the thing done, the death, and all our race. I have won; but my victory is soiled, and has no pride." He doesn't simplify his perception of the situation; he experiences the conflict as a conflict, before and after he has acted. He knows himself to be his mother's as well as his father's son. He too could not have acted differently, but he feels differently, and it is in that different feeling that the hope for communal peace resides. It is precisely this incipient remorse and guilt, responsiveness becoming full responsibility, that leads to the trial in the *Eumenides* which breaks the chain of killings and restores the social order.

In the trial itself, the defense and prosecuting attorneys, Apollo and the Furies, replicate on the level of deity the emotional extremism and imaginative rigidity which Agamemnon and Clytaemnestra exemplify. Each invokes a different kind of justice; neither will acknowledge or respect the other's rights and claims. To Apollo, god of light, prophet of Zeus, the female Furies are merely bestial subterranean creatures out for nothing more than vengeance. And though initially they describe themselves in these same terms, even after they begin to change from bloodhounds to protectresses of family order, his perception of them stays the same. They meanwhile see him and the new order of gods as infringing on their ancient rights, their immemorial primeval powers. Athena, on the other hand, continues the work which the chorus had performed in the *Agamemnon*. She is especially suited for this inclusive mediating role: as a female deity she is sympathetic to the Furies' demand for justice against the matricide, and she recognizes the power of their enmity if their demand for justice isn't met; yet as a member of the sky gods, and one, moreover, born of a father only, not a mother, she can understand the powerful obligation on Orestes to avenge his father's death. After she casts the deciding vote in favor of Orestes, she is careful to appease the Furies, offering them a home within the Athenian city-state. Athena transforms the bloodstained robe in which Agamemnon has been murdered to "the investiture of purple stained robes" which the Furies, now renamed the Eumenides, will wear, symbolizing their transformation from the subhuman creatures of vengeance to the civilized and civilizing guardians of the community.

John Herington sees the *Eumenides* as a kind of political parable, a symbolic reenactment of the social transformation taking place in Athens in the middle of the fifth century, B.C.—a transformation from an archaic, clan-dominated social order to a constitutional democracy. In Herington's view, the younger Olympian gods symbolize the Periclean progressive force of change, the human power to reform social and political orders, whereas the Furies symbolize the forces of conservatism, upholders of the ancient ways, inherited traditions, established customs. We saw a similar conflict in the Dan White trial between progressive and conservative forces. Of course the world of the *Oresteia* is religious; the social order it depicts is defined by its relation to sacred though competing claims, whereas the world of Dan White, our world, is essentially secular. These differences aside, it still seems no small irony that Dan White invoked the Furies in his campaign literature ("You must realize there are thousands upon thousands of frustrated angry people such as yourselves waiting to unleash a fury . . . "). Nor does it seem inaccurate to say that in striking down the two most prominent and powerful liberal politicians in the city, politicians who in his view were threatening the values of an older, more established conservative community, Dan White was acting with the Furies' blessing, and the Furies not only provided his defense, they also comprised the jury. Unlike Orestes, though, he never once expressed the least regret. And while no Athena intervened, in good choral fashion all that we who looked on could do was sound an ineffectual cry of outrage as the Furies carried out their vengeance under the investiture of law.

5

Directly or indirectly the ethical imagination is always asking, how should we live our lives, what should we value? At the same time it recognizes that as our circumstances change so to some extent our answers to these questions have to change as well. This recognition, however, doesn't necessarily lead to moral relativism. If we say that in the realm of moral practice there are no absolute and final certainties, we can still believe in certainties of a more local and provisional nature. Or conversely, if we say that our answers to moral questions should be conditional and open-ended we are not at the same time saying that one answer is as good as any other, or that within particular occasions there are no better or worse ways of living. The forms of western poetry may all be arbitrary cultural creations. Given these forms, however, it is possible to say that some are more capable than others as a means of understanding our experience. Imagine for a moment if Milton had tried to justify the ways of God to man in limerick stanzas, instead of blank verse paragraphs. How far would he have gotten?

> The first disobedience of man,
> Of Adam and Eve is my plan,
> How the fruit God forbid them
> To sample undid them,
> Sing Heavenly Muse once again.

It is precisely in the interests of living a better life, a life more flexibly responsive to the possibilities of being, that the ethical imagination tries to step outside even the deepest assumptions so as to turn what we know best into something strange and puzzling, thereby enabling us to see our lives, the apparent givenness and stability of our arrangements, as only a way of living, as a contingent set of possibilities always open to reform or corruption. In its allegiance to the inclusive and many-sided, the ethical imagination attempts at all times to bear witness to whatever our various orders and conventions make invisible, setting the claims of memory and tradition against the forgetfulness of the present, and the claims of the unrealized and suppressed against the past, whose effects, of course, the present bears. It has always, therefore, a political potential, particularly in its hostility to intellectual and emotional complacency, the smug ease of the absolutist, whether of the left or of the right. However, despite this potential, the ethical imagination is not reducible to politics and should not be expected to have any particular (narrowly conceived) political content. Rather, it occupies a space in and beyond culture from which the institutions and discourses of political power can be held under continual review. It is turned toward the political, in other words, but views it always from across a vital and significant distance, so as to see it clearly. Needless to say, the ethical imagination represents a power of consciousness which none of us can realize fully, or at all times. It is a power of consciousness, moreover, extremely vulnerable to the frailties and insecurities of our nature, to our need in the face of a confusing and ever more dangerous world to seek the narrow refuge of some exclusive program, or some comforting nostalgia, or the illusory stability of what often passes for "traditional values." Like the chorus in the *Agamemnon*, it defends the impure, heterogeneous, and tense condition of the human against the equally human temptation for the unambiguous and pure.

Dan White was the voice and agent of one kind of purity. To the like-minded citizens who sat in judgment on him, he represented a nostalgia for the tribal world of small communities unsullied by the abrasive mixtures of race, religion, sexual preference, or political values—a world which, of course, never existed, except on the level of their desire. If, as I suggest, the judicial process may frequently function as the legal equivalent of the open and ongoing inquiry which the ethical imagination exercises in the realm of art, the Dan White trial shows how easily corruptible that spirit of flexibility can be, that its weakness—its vulnerability—is inextricably bound up with its very strength.

Given the constraints and complexities of our attachments and needs, few of us can get through life without facing at one time or another the serious moral choices which the characters in *Billy Budd* and the *Oresteia* face. No amount of vigilance can prevent situations from arising in which one loyalty clashes with another, in which no

matter how we act we violate a sacred trust. To most of us, the way of
Agamemnon is easier psychologically than the way of Orestes or Vere.
Like Agamemnon, we try to eliminate these moral tensions by denying
on the level of emotion the claim we choose against. If Orestes or Vere
is closer to the moral ideal, if their ethical imagination is keener than
Agamemnon's, a measure of that keenness is the pain it causes, the
tragic recognition it compels. *Billy Budd* also suggests that situations
arise that are inimical to the ethical imagination, situations like war
or political upheaval, which don't permit the careful and humane dis-
criminations that are central, in my view, to the literary arts. At such
times, what the ethical imagination tries to do is to remind us of what
the times have sacrificed. We see this in some of Yeats's political
poems: In "Easter 1916," for instance, we see how even the celebra-
tion of political martyrdom does not preclude the acknowledgment
that fanaticism, even for a worthy cause, can make "a stone of the
heart." It is the ethical imagination that sees and feels both the terror
and the beauty in the "terrible beauty" that is born. And in reading
and living with the poem we come to see and feel it too.

Art, of course, is not immune to extremism and rigidity of thought
and feeling. Within the modernist movement, the tendencies toward
"pure art" on the one hand, and art engagé on the other, represent
two attempts at eliminating the ethical imagination from the aesthetic
domain. The poem as pure image or pure symbol in isolation from
quotidian experience, and the poem as handmaiden of ideological
commitment, offer us poetic versions of the moral simplifications we
see in the *Oresteia*. They effect a similar escape from the tensions and
impurities that face us in our daily lives. This is not to say, though,
that Imagism as a movement, to take one example, didn't help rejuve-
nate the art of poetry. In abandoning the stale conventions of high
Victorian Romanticism, the Imagist experiment made it possible to
write a poetry more flexibly attuned to sensory experience. It puri-
fied in order to renew. At the same time, in its exclusive preoccupa-
tion with attenuated flashes of perception, its confinement to a slen-
der band of linguistic and experiential possibilities, its aversion to
discursiveness of any kind, Imagism also entailed a moral cost; it
purified itself of moral substance. One could make an analogous
argument even about an opposite of Imagist poetry, the "protest"
poetry inspired by the Spanish Civil War, or more recently by the
Vietnam War. I'm not suggesting here that poetry should not address
itself to social and political injustices, or that in treating subjects of a

more public nature the political verse of the thirties and sixties didn't help extend the range of what poetry can say or do. But insofar as such verse fails to do imaginative justice to the injustices it calls attention to, insofar as it indulges in a self-applauding show of moral outrage, or relies on slogans and formulae, blunting its power of discrimination out of loyalty to some political agenda, such verse will never rise above its topical appeal. However important or necessary Imagism or poetry in service to a cause may seem now from a literary-historical point of view, the poems that adhere exclusively to Imagist principles or ideological allegiance can have at best only an ephemeral claim upon our moral being, for the equipment that they offer is insufficient for the dangers in us and around us. We turn to literary works like the *Oresteia* and *Billy Budd* for the ethical imagination they embody, the moral problems they enact and understand, problems which turn us back toward life, if no less vulnerable to life's uncertainties, then a little less prone to error, because a little more alert to what we are, to what can happen.

1989

In Praise of the Impure:
Narrative Consciousness in Poetry

There is no poem in the realm of autonomy as there is no story or narrative. Narrative is produced by, and repeats, the situation of the impeded will, the will subject to a law other than its own, subject to antinomic laws. Narrative is omnipresent in poetry. Because all speaking is action which has a history.
—Allen Grossman, *Summa Lyrica*

1

When we talk about narrative in poetry, we usually have in mind the ordinary sense of storytelling as an explicit account of some external action with a beginning, middle, and end. While narrative in this sense has become increasingly important for many poets of my generation as a way of giving to their work a wider range of interest and appeal, there is a deeper narrative expression which is either overlooked in our discussions, or confused with the more commonplace notions of narrative as mere anecdote.

Narrative in the more fundamental sense has to do with implicit social, psychological, and linguistic actions in which words, sentences and poetic forms, as well as the particular subjects they illuminate, comprise part of a historical continuum in relation to which the speaking self is defined. This kind of narrative, as Allen Grossman observes, is omnipresent in poetry; it is impure, mongrel, not confined to any one genre or style. As I hope to show, it is seldom absent even from poetry that is avowedly antinarrative.

We have difficulty making this distinction, though, because for over seventy-five years an aesthetic of radical subjectivity has placed narrative in general (along with meter) under a kind of unofficial ban. Until quite recently, most poets and readers of poetry have assumed that narrative conventions, like conventional schemes of any kind, inhibit individual expression: according to this view, to be true to the irreducible uniqueness of personal experience entails either avoiding or violating all predetermined forms and discursive structures. Behind much of the experimental poetry of the sixties and seventies is a vision of the self as existing prior to its social and historical affilia tions. What community does exist in the work of Deep Image poets, say, derives not from the external world of ordinary experience but from the internal world of the collective unconscious where the self in solitude, transcending the false consciousness of cultural norms, regains a precultural wholeness. If the rejection of narrative in Deep Image poetics expresses or follows from a rejection of time, of the unfolding of the self in history, in favor of the changelessness of myth, an emerging interest in narrative procedures can be seen as a desire to move beyond the private experience of the isolated self and establish contact with the lives of others, with the social world and with the past.

Certainly not all the experimental poets of the sixties and seventies were as thoroughly ahistorical as the poets associated with Deep Image. Yet the same distrust of abstract design as an obstacle to self-expression can be found in poets as different as Lowell, Duncan, Ginsberg, Rich, and Ashbery. In varying degrees, these poets also subscribe to a poetics of radical subjectivity. Underlying and ratifying their assumption that convention is inherently repressive is the more general assumption that authentic selfhood can be recovered only in opposition to certain shared norms of cultural practice.

There was nothing new or original about this contemporary commitment to the unique and autonomous self. The arguments on behalf of free verse and immediacy of presentation, and against all predetermined schemes, including narrative arrangement, derives, at least in our century, from the early moderns. In 1914 in his essay on Imagism, Ford Madox Ford rejected all verse "cut to a pattern" on the grounds that it inevitably "sacrifices a certain amount . . . of the personality of the writer." Free verse, on the other hand, "allows a freer play for self-expression than even narrative prose; at the same time it calls for an even greater precision in that self-expression." Likewise, T. E. Hulme in his 1908 lecture on modern poetry based his rejection of both meter and epic subjects on the grounds that modernity had undermined all absolute truths that might sustain a public discourse. Modern poetry "has become definitely and finally introspective and deals with expression and communication of momentary phases of the poet's mind. . . . In the arts, we seek for the maximum of individual and personal expression, rather than for the attainment of any absolute beauty."

A similar feeling that narrative composition and self-expression are mutually exclusive can be found even among those artists ostensibly concerned with grounding artistic authority upon a more objective basis. In an unpublished essay entitled "The Use of Poetry," William Carlos Williams defines the imagination as a fragmenting power which sharpens our sense perception by divesting objects of conventional meaning. He wonderfully compares the special character of this imaginative act to "the much greater interest felt in the snatches of pictures shown at the movies between the regular films, to advertise pictures coming the following week, than the regular features themselves. The experience is of something much more vivid and much more sensual than the entire film will be. It is because the banality of sequence has been removed." Putting aside the question of whether anyone would pay twenty-five cents, or seven dollars, to see two hours of previews, we can see how for Williams narrative sequence is synonymous with all the conventional contexts and associations which accrue to objects and which prevent us from seeing them freshly, in their sensual immediacy, as unique autonomous structures. Williams' aversion to what he thought of as the banality of sequence parallels the aversion to narrative representation among the modern painters: as Wassily Kandinsky puts it in his famous essay, "The Spiritual in Art" (1912), "We must find a form which excludes a fairy-tale effect and which does not hinder pure color action. To this end, form, movement, color, natural and imaginary objects must be divorced from any narrative intent." Narrative, in other words, has to do with things seen in relation to the purposes they ordinarily serve, whereas modernist art attempts to see objects purely as objects, liberated from the taint of all extraneous utility.

This seeming aesthetic of things, however, is no less individualistic than Ford's or Hulme's concern for self-expression. For what the artist discovers when he looks at things "cleared of their stubborn man-locked set" is the origin of whatever sensations moved him to notice them in the first place. Value comes ultimately not from material objects but from the primacy of individual perception. The ultimate ground of Stieglitz's theory of equivalents, or Eliot's objective correlative, or Williams's notion of contact with the local as the test of art, is the subjective sensibility of the perceiving artist whose avowed autonomy from all social obligation or convention is mirrored in the autonomous objects of his gaze.

Narrative frames, traditional prosodies, discursive language, even syntax itself, were regarded by the early moderns as different facets of a single network of abstraction which cut the self off from the richness of individual perception. In promoting a subjectivist aesthetic based on the immediate perception of specific images, these artists were attempting to resist not just the dead weight of their Victorian past but the standardizing pressures of the modern present. Art became, in their view, the last refuge of the individual in an increasingly centralized society, socially organized by large-scale bureaucracies and the working conditions of mass production—a society where the levelings of mass culture threatened the integrity of the expressive self.

In retrospect, these techniques of dissociation and the individualism they are meant to safeguard seem less a resistance to the modern world than a mirror image of it. American Modernism is roughly coincident with the rise of a national advertising industry whose function was to generate consumers for the flood of goods our industries were producing at incredible speed. The corporate world regarded all traditional patterns of life which resisted the imperatives of an emerging consumer culture as "puritanism in consumption": "Advertising," as Leverett S. Lyon put it in his contribution to *The Encyclopedia of the Social Sciences* during the twenties, "is the greatest force at work against the traditional economy of an age-long poverty as well as that of our own pioneer period; it is almost the only force at work against puritanism in consumption. It can infuse art into the things of life; and it will. . . . " Commercial modernism, like aesthetic modernism, placed exclusive value in nullifying "the customs of ages," so as to make the consumer more receptive to "the ever evolving new." Moreover, there is a disquieting parallel between the desire of artists to strip objects of any coherent context in the name of immediacy of perception and the desire of business to make commodities more appealing by dissociating them from the conditions under which they were produced. The Poundian ideal of the image flash which liberates the mind from the constraints of time and space resembles the ideal of the advertised commodity, which in the words of one advertising executive is "to release people from the limitations of their own lives." The Poundian image is designed, of course, to illuminate the mind, not manipulate it for financial gain. My point in comparing the rhetoric of early advertising with the rhetoric of early modernist aesthetic theory is to show that the captains of industry and the captains of art had more in common than the artists themselves suspected. Successful advertising copy, like early modern notions of successful art, was antitraditional, anticritical, nondiscursive, nondidactic, entirely an appeal to instincts, feelings, and sense perceptions. As Walter Dill Scott puts it in *Influencing Men in Business* (1911): "The man with the proper imagination is able to conceive of any commodity in such a way that it becomes an object of emotion to him and to those to whom he imparts his picture, and hence creates desire rather than a mere feeling of ought." (See Stuart Ewen's *Captains of Consciousness*, New York: McGraw-Hill, 1976.)

Many of the modernists, of course, came to feel the limitations of their early theories. Williams and Pound both attempted to develop poetic forms that would enable them to include and accommodate the heterogeneous materials of history. Pound even conceived of the *Cantos* in narrative terms, as "the shape of a journey which begins 'In the Dark Forest,' crosses the Purgatory of human error, and ends in the light." Yet both he and Williams, early and late, in theory if not always in practice, remained distrustful of the discursive, syntactic, narrative connections that might enact the movement of a mind through the stages of thinking, preferring instead the imagistic method of wedging image next to image, historical fragment next to historical fragment. The method of the *Cantos* for the most part undercuts the ambition it is meant to serve, and the poem does not "cohere."

On the other hand, the best poems by Williams, Eliot, and Pound are never entirely nondiscursive, antinarrative, or fragmentary. The images pure and simple of an open doorway and a maple leaf mean nothing until they are specifically connected to a world of history and grief. That is why in "Ars Poetica," one of the great unintentionally comic poems of the world, Archibald MacLeish is forced to tell us what each and every image means even as he says he shouldn't have to. To the extent that "The Love Song of J. Alfred Prufrock," *Four Quartets*, or *The Waste Land*, books 1 and 2 of *Paterson*, or the Pisan *Cantos* enact the mind in action as it attempts to clarify its historical position in the world, they carry on, by necessity, illicit relations with traditional elements of narrative.

Take, for example, Williams's justly famous poem, "By the Road to the Contagious Hospital," the first poem from *Spring and All*, one of his most experimental books:

> By the road to the contagious hospital
> under the surge of the blue

mottled clouds driven from the
northeast—a cold wind. Beyond, the
waste of broad, muddy fields
brown with dried weeds, standing and fallen

patches of standing water
the scattering of tall trees

All along the road the reddish
purplish, forked, upstanding, twiggy
stuff of bushes and small trees
with dead, brown leaves under them
leafless vines—

Lifeless in appearance, sluggish
dazed spring approaches—

They enter the new world naked,
cold, uncertain of all
save that they enter. All about them
the cold, familiar wind—

Now the grass, tomorrow
the stiff curl of wildcarrot leaf
One by one objects are defined—
It quickens: clarity, outline of leaf

But now the stark dignity of
entrance—Still, the profound change
has come upon them: rooted, they
grip down and begin to awaken

The poem overall has the shape of a story, moving as it does from
death to life, atomistic stasis to concerted motion, from description of
discrete details to comprehension of things in complex and living rela-
tion to each other, in which the one and the many, the whole and the
parts that compose it, are mutually implicated and mutually sustain-
ing. As the story unfolds, moreover, the style itself changes in
response to the changing narrative. In the pre-spring landscape of the
opening three stanzas, the landscape's atomistic lifelessness is quietly

suggested by the flat, merely descriptive language on the one hand
and by the series of sentence fragments on the other ("patches of
standing water / the scattering of tall trees"). When spring approach-
es, though, not only do verbs appear, joining object to object, but the
language also moves from mere physical description to something
more abstract and conceptual: "Lifeless in appearance, sluggish /
dazed spring approaches— / They enter the new world naked. . . . "
The lines are as much about a change of aesthetic as they are about a
change of season. One can read in them a kind of tacit critique of the
imagist poet's exclusive delight in the mere appearance of things, in
the surfaces of sense perception. The understanding sees the meta-
physical approach of spring where the eye sees only lifelessness.
(These lines, in effect, look forward to "The Yachts," Williams's other
great critique of an exclusively objectivist aesthetic, a poem in which
the eye's delight in the sensuous appearance of the yachts ["mothlike
in mists"] is undercut by the mind's ability to see through that
appearance to the social and political injustices which sustain it.)

As Williams moves beyond the sensory (without entirely abandon-
ing it), he draws on a wide array of linguistic and rhetorical
resources, some of which modernist literary theory had proscribed,
including ideas, abstractions, personifications ("dazed spring
approaches," "They enter . . . naked, / cold, uncertain"), puns ("It
quickens," "the profound change"), as well as the narrative shape
implicit in the syntactical shifts from passive to active construction to
suggest the passive and active nature of the changes he describes
("objects are defined— / It quickens"). The more complex language
reflects a more complex vision, capable of defining objects in a kind of
nominalistic purity at the same time that it connects objects to each
other as different manifestations of the same general process. The
exuberant energy of Williams's attention is expressed more through
the syntactic arrangement of the lines than through the images. In
fact, there are surprisingly few images in the second half of the poem.
But notice how the arc of perception enacted by the sequence of
clauses swings in chiasmatic order between general and particular
terms. No sooner is spring invoked as an abstract entity than it
changes into the collectivity of new growth—"they enter the new
world"—which, in turn, is differentiated further into "grass," then
into "the stiff curl of wildcarrot leaf"; then back again through gener-
ic "objects" to the abstract force ("It") which "quickens" them. The
story played out by these stylistic changes, the turns and shifts of dic-

tion and syntax, dramatize the excitement and struggle of a mind participating in the birth it witnesses. By means of syntax the poem enacts the process of its own emergence in and through the emergence of spring.

There are also, however, extrinsic stories at work in our appreciation of the poem. "By the Road to the Contagious Hospital" is a modern pastoral. An important dimension of its meaning depends in part on our ability to situate the poem in relation to the pastoral tradition, to read it as a new chapter in the narrative of that tradition.

If most pastorals are set in some Arcadian landscape, Williams sets his by a hospital, on a barren stretch of land, where disease and waste are inescapably associated with the world into which new life will come. And while most spring poems idealize renewal, Williams sees renewal in terms of pain, struggle, vulnerability, and resilience. Williams also adapts and reworks the messianic strain of the pastoral tradition, the classic exemplar of which is Virgil's "Fourth Eclogue." Virgil imagines the reestablishment of the Golden Age in an idealized future while Williams suggests that the Golden Age is, as Peter Schmidt observes, "continually lost, found, and lost again." (See *William Carlos Williams, the Arts, and Literary Tradition*, Baton Rouge: Louisiana State University Press, 1988.) In playing against the expectations implicit in the tradition he inherits, Williams continues that tradition, adapting the story of it to the new conditions of the American scene. And of course there is also the subplot of the poem as an answer to *The Waste Land*, which, Williams believed, had dealt a catastrophic blow to American letters. Eliot's internationalism and traditionalism, his ironic contrast of physical renewal and spiritual impoverishment, are countered in the closing lines of Williams's poem by the interweaving of moral and erotic abstractions—"the stark dignity of entrance," "the profound change"—with the physical action of gripping down and awakening, thereby investing the physical regeneration with a metaphysical, anti-Eliotic significance.

The poem, in other words, is not an autonomous structure, a purely sensory presentation of a landscape. It is rather an implied story within a matrix of stories whose intersecting arcs embrace the social and literary conditions (and this includes the past as well as the present) within which the poem was written, and within which the poem is read. But to view the poem this way is to violate many of the dichotomies so prominent in the literary theories Williams himself espouses (between past and present, tradition and self-expression, ideas and things), dichotomies which we have inherited and which have blinded us, I think, to the theory-defying richness of the work itself.

2

It should be clear from the opening section that I am not at all concerned with narrative poetry but rather with the narrative elements in poetry of any kind. I regard narrative as having more to do with a particular activity of consciousness than with technical matters, or with anecdote, or with the mere sequentiality of external happenings. Narrative involves what W. S. Di Piero calls "states of becoming," the enactment as well as imitation of action (mental or physical, emotional or intellectual) in the unfolding of the verse. The complete rendering of an action implies an arc connecting origins and ends—how I have come to do this (past) is implicit in what I am doing (present), and what I am doing is unintelligible apart from what I am doing it for (future). Anything in the poem which clarifies or contributes to the rendering of this action has narrative meaning. Thus it is possible to talk about meter or syntax as narrative elements, and about how the evolving shape of a sentence, for instance, or the developing contour of a particular rhythm, forms a segment of the arc which the poem as a whole describes.

"Those Winter Sundays," by Robert Hayden, is a case in point. This is a lyric poem about the belated recognition of value as a son recalls regretfully all the father's unappreciated acts of kindness:

> Sundays too my father got up early
> and put his clothes on in the blueblack cold,
> then with cracked hands that ached
> from labor in the weekday weather made
> banked fires blaze. No one ever thanked him.
>
> I'd wake and hear the cold splintering, breaking.
> When the rooms were warm, he'd call,
> and slowly I would rise and dress,
> fearing the chronic angers of that house,
>
> Speaking indifferently to him,
> who had driven out the cold

and polished my good shoes as well.
What did I know, what did I know
of love's austere and lonely offices?

The whole poem turns on the word "too" in the opening line which points beyond the particular action of the father's early rising to the larger context of his hard life as an outdoor laborer. The weaving together of family and work, the chronic angers of that house and the general conditions outside the house which contribute to that anger, and which make the recollection of the small unacknowledged acts of care so poignant, is continued in the structure of the succeeding clauses. The long noun clause beginning "then with cracked hands that ached . . ." tells us why the hands are aching before describing what the hands are doing. By interposing that contextual detail between the noun and verb, Hayden manages retrospectively to integrate a description of the father's Sunday ritual with the speaker's present recognition of the sacrifice and pain involved in it, a recognition he was incapable of as a child.

Throughout the poem Hayden tells two stories at the same time: the story of the conflict between the father and son, and the story of the conflict within the speaker between a recollecting self whose horizon of vision and sympathy is wide, and a recollected experiencing self whose horizon of vision and sympathy is extremely narrow. The narrative artistry appears not in the imagery, which as in "By the Road to the Contagious Hospital" is apt without being especially striking; but rather in the movement of the sentences as they shift almost seamlessly back and forth between these two perspectives. The penultimate sentence, for instance, drawn over several lines, enacts both the estrangements of the past and the present feeling of connection: it isolates the father and son by placing their actions on separate lines, and yet it joins the two together by making them parts of a single sentence. The rhythm too participates in this drama, shifting as the perspective shifts. The regularity of the opening two lines, alternating between trochaic and iambic cadences, suggests the daily, repetitive nature of the father's loving attentions. When the sentence moves beyond the household to account for why the cracked hands ached, the alliteration and heavy stresses roughen the cadence to suggest the speaker's present knowledge of "love's austere and lonely offices," and of the social and economic conditions which inform and constrain that love.

3

A commitment to narrative presupposes that feeling is unintelligible apart from source or motive on the one hand, and destination or purpose on the other. Which is to say, the complete articulation of feeling implies a movement, not a stasis, an arising from as well as a going toward. This movement, moreover, can take any number of forms, from the linear unfolding of dormancy to waking in "By the Road to the Contagious Hospital," to the spiraling backward motion in "Those Winter Sundays" from present regret to past estrangement, from effect to cause. In whatever direction, the life of narrative begins with the desire to move between states of feeling so as to understand and articulate the community of relations which obtains when the poet asks why, as well as how, he feels. As such, he commits himself to a poetry of discrimination and judgment which does not exclude intensity of feeling but does subordinate that intensity to the tracing of the larger context within which it evolves.

Those who distrust narrative organization will counter that all feeling, and certainly the most profound feeling, is ultimately indeterminate, and that the "closure" of narrative forms inevitably falsifies the "radical openness" of life. This argument, however, depends on a rigid dichotomy between form and process, openness and closure, and a tacitly absolutist moral program that regards openness as an a priori good, and closure as an a priori evil. Yet closure and openness are relative effects that are mutually entailing, not mutually exclusive. In the particular words and sentences one chooses, in the establishment of verb tense, voice or context, even the most radically open text has closure, closing off certain possibilities of meaning by raising others. As Wayne Booth points out, "Total openness is total entropy—and hence total apathy for a reader." Moreover, there is nothing inherently "subversive" or "authoritarian" about either closed or open structures. The political effect of either depends on the extraliterary context of the work itself. The experimental openness of much Eastern European literature is made politically meaningful only in relation to the closed authoritarian societies within which that work is produced. In a culture such as ours in which consumerism seems to be the primary goal of life, openness to each and every indeterminate meaning and experience carries a more complicated (one might even say more indeterminate) moral valence.

Besides, to say that feeling is ultimately indeterminate is not to say
that it is indefinable, at least not in its less-than-ultimate interests,
modes and relations. That we can with some consensus distinguish
the sentimental from what Keats called "the true voice of feeling" sug-
gests an ability to discriminate and judge the feelings we express. This
is not to say that the poet can always answer the question why he feels
the way he does, only that the asking of it is fundamental to the nar-
rative act. Narrative, in other words, commits the poet to neither clo-
sure nor openness but to some always-changing relation between the
two; it is the movement of mind in the act of questioning; it is the
"quest," so to speak, in questioning—the looking for, if not the find-
ing.

On a larger scale than in "Those Winter Sundays," "Combat" by
C. K. Williams sets in motion a more complicated drama of perspec-
tive between a recollecting and experiencing self. "Combat" is less
lyrical and more meditative than either "By the Road to the Conta-
gious Hospital" or "Those Winter Sundays." And as part of its loos-
er meditative structure it draws more amply on narrative resources as
a way of making sense of the self in relation to the various historical
pressures that have shaped it.

The poem concerns a beautiful German girl with whom the speak-
er was involved when he was twenty-one, and her silent mother. Most
of the drama takes place in the speaker's consciousness as he revisits
in memory the two sites in the girl's apartment where "everything that
mattered happened": the bedroom "down the book-lined corridor"
where he and Moira engaged in a kind of sexual combat without ever
consummating the relationship, and the living room where Moira
would massage the mother's misshapen "frightening yellow" feet while
telling the boy, over and over, the same stories of their escape from
Germany, and of her father's suicide. The opening description of the
apartment quietly invests it with symbolic meaning, so that it becomes
a kind of historical microcosm, in which the contradictions of the
recent past, of the war and its aftermath, its racial violence and cul-
tural guilt, are played out in miniature:

> Lovely Moira! Could I ever have forgotten you? No,
>   not forgotten, only not had with me for a time
>   that dark, slow voice, those vulnerable eyes, those
>   ankles finely tendoned as a thoroughbred's .

. . . .

The mother, I remember, was so white, not all that old
    but white: everything, hair, skin, lips, was ash,
except her feet, which Moira would often hold on her
    lap to massage and which were a deep,
frightening yellow, the skin thickened and dense,
    horned with calluses and chains of coarse, dry
    bunions,
the nails deformed and brown, so deeply buried that
    they looked like chips of tortoiseshell.
Moira would rub the poor, sad things, twisting and
    kneading at them with her strong hands;
the mother's eyes would be closed, occasionally she'd
    mutter something under her breath in German.
That was their language—they were, Moira said,
    refugees, but the word didn't do them justice.
They were well-off, very much so, their apartment
    was, in fact, the most splendid thing I'd ever
    seen.
There were lithographs and etchings—some Klees, I
    think; a Munch—a lot of very flat oriental rugs,
voluptuous leather furniture and china so frail the
    molds were surely cast from butterflies.
I never found out how they'd brought it all with
    them: what Moira told me was of displaced-person
    camps,
a pilgrimage on foot from Prussia and the Russians,
    then Frankfurt, Rotterdam, and here, "freedom."
. . . .
what was most important to her at that age was her
    father, who she'd hardly known and who'd just
    died.
He was a general, she told me, the chief of staff or
    something of "the war against the Russians."
He'd been one of the conspirators against Hitler and
    when the plot failed he'd committed suicide,
all of which meant not very much to me, however
    good the story was (and I heard it often),
because people then were still trying to forget the
    war, it had been almost ignored, even in school,
and I had no context much beyond what my childhood

comic books had given me to hang any of it on.

This passage introduces details the speaker will return to, each time with greater comprehension as he places his adolescent self in relation to the historical forces he was blind to at the time and yet which choreographed almost everything he felt, did, and perceived. Everything in the apartment isolates the mother and daughter from the speaker. The apartment itself, its exquisite furnishings and high-cultural artifacts, its "book-lined corridor," stands in contrast to the boy whose knowledge of history derives primarily from "comic books." And yet the air of refinement implicit in their possessions is complicated by the stories Moira tells about her and her mother's pilgrimage to "freedom," their old life in Germany, and her father's involvement in the plot to assassinate Hitler.

Ironically, as Moira's stories grow more detailed, more poignant, the boy grows more distracted, "hardly listening anyway by then, one hand on a thigh, the other stroking, / with such compassion, such generous concern, such cunning twenty-one-year-old commiseration, / her hair, her perfect hair, then the corner of her mouth, then, so far away, the rich rim of a breast."

> . . . I was so distracted that I couldn't even get their
>   name right:
> . . . .
> and Moira's little joke before she'd let me take her
>   clothes off was that we'd have lessons, "Von C . . . "
>   "No, Von C . . . "
> Later, when I was studying the holocaust, I found it
>   again, the name, Von C. . . , in Shirer's *Reich*:
> it had, indeed, existed, and it had, yes, somewhere
>   on the Eastern front, blown its noble head off.
> I wasn't very moved. I wasn't in that city anymore,
>   I'd ceased long before ever to see them,
> and besides, I'd changed by then—I was more aware
>   of history and was beginning to realize,
> however tardily, that one's moral structures tended
>   to be air unless you grounded them in real
>   events.
> Everything I did learn seemed to negate something
>   else, everything was more or less up for grabs,

but the war, the Germans, all I knew about that
    now—no, never: what a complex triumph to
    have a nation,
all of it, beneath you, what a splendid culmination
    for the adolescence of one's ethics!

The irony with which he earlier circumscribes his adolescent long-
ing (hardly listening to her story while his hand strokes with "such com-
passion, such generous concern . . . her hair, her perfect hair . . . "), he
now exercises on his later, newly awakened ethical awareness. The
passage is crucial, though, for the poem is really about the poet's eth-
ical maturation, which culminates in the complicated and inclusive
vision that the poem overall enacts. If as a boy he sees Moira narcis-
sistically only as an object of desire, and then later, with no less nar-
cissism, as an object of condescension ("I reformulated her—them—
forgave them, held them fondly, with a heavy lick of condescension, in
my system"—as if his ethical adolescence were just a slight sublima-
tion of his adolescent sexuality), he now begins to see her and her
mother in a much more baffling and nuanced light. Ethical maturity,
he implies, consists not in the mechanical and self-serving act of plac-
ing people in one's "system," in having "a nation, all of it, beneath
you"; rather, it consists in the ability to open up the past to question-
ing. While Moira seems more beautiful now in memory than she did
when he was a boy "and quibbled everything," he can also see now
what escaped him then, that there were "promises of dimness, vaults
and hidden banks of coolness" in the way she engineered his sexual
advances, imitating all the sounds and gestures of lovemaking "while
nothing would be happening, nothing, that is, in the way I'd mean it
now." Now as he broods over the scene, "the three of us in place, the
conversation that seemed sometimes like ritual, eternally recurring,"
he brings more and more external history to bear on how he sees him-
self in relation to these women:

It's strange now, doing it again, the business of the
    camps and slaughters, the quick flicker of outrage
that hardly does its work anymore, all the carnage,
    all our own omissions interposed,
then those two, in their chambers, correct, aristocratic,
    even with the old one's calcifying feet
and the younger one's intensities—those eyes that

pierce me still from that far back with jolts of
    longing.
I frame the image: the two women, the young man,
    they, poised, gracious, he smoldering with impatience,
and I realize I've never really asked myself what
    could she, or they, possibly have wanted of me?
What am I doing in that room, a teacup trembling on
    my knee, that odd, barbed name mangled in my
    mouth?

The long sentence that begins this passage brings all of the ele-
ments of the poem together in an arc which moves from the historical
to the personal, from the camps and slaughters to the girl, and ironi-
cally from lesser to greater intensity of feeling, from the faint flicker
of outrage at the Holocaust "that hardly does its work anymore," to
Moira's eyes "that pierce me still from that far back with jolts of long-
ing." If it is a measure of the speaker's integrity as a witness of his
own experience to admit that personal memory is more moving than
secondhand historical knowledge, even of genocide, the memory itself
is still inextricably bound up with history. It is precisely the personal
and public history held in that long sentence which enables the speak-
er now to frame the image of himself with Moira and her mother, and
which enables him to ask for the first time: "what could she, or they,
possibly have wanted of me?"

What I come to now, running over it again, I think I
    want to keep as undramatic as I can.
These revisions of the past are probably even less
    trustworthy than our random, everyday assemblages
and have most likely even more to do with present
    unknowables, so I offer this almost in passing,
with nothing, no moral distillation, no headily press-
    ing imperatives meant to be lurking beneath it.
I wonder, putting it most simply, leaving out humiliation,
    anything like that, if I might have been their Jew?
I wonder, I mean, if I might have been an implement
    for them, . . .

. . . .
. . . of absolution, what they'd have used to get them
    shed of something rankling—history, it would be . . . .

The syntax with all its hedging qualifications dramatizes the hesitant, speculative and even reluctant process by which the mind arrives at this particular answer. It also illustrates an almost fastidious care for accuracy, for defining as precisely as Williams can such elusive feelings; part of the precision, too, involves acknowledging that he can never know for certain if his revisions of the past are true.

> The mother, what I felt from her, that bulk of
>   silence, that withholding that I read as sorrow:
> might it have been instead the heroic containment of
>   a probably reflexive loathing of me?
> How much, no matter what their good intentions (of
>   which from her I had no evidence at all)
> and even with the liberal husband (although the generals'
>   reasons weren't that pure and got there very
>   late),
> how much must they have inevitably absorbed, that
>   Nazi generation, those Aryan epochs?
> And if the mother shuddered, what would Moira
>   have gone through with me spinning at her nipple,
> her own juices and the inept emissions I'd splatter on
>   her gluing her to me?
> The purifying Jew . . . .

The judgment that animates these lines is a complicated mixture of admiration and contempt. By establishing the historical pressures which inform Moira's and her mother's attitudes and actions, Williams is able to perceive an almost heroic dimension to the mother's silence without at the same time excusing the racism he imagines might be implicit in it. And yet he cannot revise his understanding of their motives without revising his understanding of his own. What until this point appears as the callow self-absorption of adolescent sexuality, his desire to have from Moira "what I had to have," now takes on a more sinister and more humiliating cast. As "the purifying Jew," the speaker realizes he was all along a figure in their history, with the disquieting implication that he may have sensed this and in his infatuation "gone along with them anyway":

> All the indignities I let be perpetrated on me while I
>   lolled in that luxurious detention:

could I really have believed they only had to do with
 virtue, maidenhood, or even with, I remember
 thinking—
I came this close—some intricate attempt Moira
 might be making to redeem a slight on the part of
 the mother?
Or might inklings have arisen and might I, in my
 infatuation, have gone along with them anyway?
I knew something, surely: I'd have had to. What I
 really knew, of course, I'll never know again.
Beautiful memory, most precious and most treacherous
 sister: what temples must we build for you.
And even then, how belatedly you open to us; even
 then, with what exuberance you cross us.

I want to offer here, "almost in passing . . . with no moral distillation . . . lurking beneath it," that the speaker's vulnerability to this sort of manipulation and self-deception is a function more of his American Jewishness than of his Jewishness per se, of his being a product of a culture that was "still trying to forget the war," someone whose knowledge of the war came primarily from "childhood comic books." His characteristically American ignorance of history—his own as well as Moira's—facilitated his participation in her historical drama.

The long lines and longer, almost fussily elaborated sentences that shift continually throughout the poem from adolescent to adult perspective, from Moira and the boy to Moira and the mother, from description to speculation, from scene to context, present to past, simultaneously enable the speaker both to reconstruct the past and to call the act of reconstruction into question. "Memory" is treacherous insofar as "our revisions of the past" are conditioned by "present unknowables," by the fluid relations of public and private history, much of which is either inaccessible or belatedly accessible to consciousness. Yet memory is also precious; it is all we have to track our personal and cultural evolution. The commitment to a faithful rendering of the past, together with the understanding that such renderings are unreliable, is the ultimate expression of the speaker's ethical maturity. We see ourselves as we are now in and through the quality of attention enacted in our stories of the past. Hence, the need both for the "closure" of a frame and for the openness of speculation that can question what the frame distorts or excludes.

If one were to rewrite "Combat" according to an Imagist or Deep Image aesthetic, removing "the banality of sequence" in favor of the nondiscursive, nonnarrative presentation of discrete sense impressions and fragments of memory, one would destroy the poem's life. As the poem unfolds, the big lines, the flexible language comprising images and abstractions, high diction and low, and the long sentences moving so restlessly through the lines, all trace the mental action of sorting through, testing, and discriminating the materials of experience with the energy of thought. The image may well be the most expressive and intense feature of poetry, and a poetry composed purely of discontinuous images may achieve a degree of intensity not available to poems like "Combat." Yet what such poetry gains in intensity it loses in the power to weigh and determine the significance of what it presents. Finally, to say that images are the most intense elements of poetry is not to say that other elements are any less important. As A. C. Bradley once remarked, refuting Poe's belief that a long narrative poem wasn't, strictly speaking, poetry, "Naturally, in any poem not quite short, there must be many variations and grades of poetic intensity; but to represent the differences of these numerous grades as a simple antithesis between pure poetry and mere prose is like saying that, because the eyes are the most expressive part of the face, the rest of the face expresses nothing. To hold, again, that this variation of intensity is a defect is like holding that a face would be more beautiful if it were all eyes. . . ."

4

"By the Road to the Contagious Hospital," "Those Winter Sundays," and "Combat" illustrate in different ways my second definition of narrative as the implicit stylistic and thematic stories enacted by the language and movement of the verse. Though this deeper sense of narrative is also present in Elizabeth Bishop's "The Moose," this poem is distinguished from the others by making storytelling itself an important part of its subject. "The Moose" is a poem of stories as well as a poem about stories, or more precisely, about how even when the stories we tell are fraught with "deaths, deaths and sicknesses," there is still something in the communal act of telling stories that is life-affirming and life-sustaining.

As in "Combat," very little happens in the poem. Beyond the
startling appearance of the moose in the concluding lines, the drama
here is reflected in the speaker's perception of the changing landscape
seen from the window of a bus as it journeys east to west, from Nova
Scotia through New Brunswick, and in the interplay between the nar-
rative frame which the bus journey provides, and the stories which
the speaker overhears. In effect, Bishop establishes two narrative
movements—the literal movement of the bus (which is also a move-
ment from the known to the unknown, and temporally speaking from
present to future), and the countermovement enacted by the stories,
from west to east, present to past, strangeness to familiarity.

> From narrow provinces
> of fish and bread and tea,
> home of the long tides
> where the bay leaves the sea
> twice a day and takes
> the herrings long rides,
>
> where if the river
> enters or retreats
> in a wall of brown foam
> depends on if it meets
> the bay coming in,
> the bay not at home;
>
> where, silted red,
> sometimes the sun sets
> facing a red sea,
> and others, veins the flats'
> lavender, rich mud
> in burning rivulets;
>
> on red, gravelly roads,
> down rows of sugar maples,
> past clapboard farmhouses
> and neat, clapboard churches,
> bleached, ridged as clamshells,
> past twin silver birches,

> through late afternoon
> a bus journeys west . . .

The description indicates the speaker's intimate relation to the place she's leaving. The mundane human elements ("provinces / of fish and bread and tea") modulate into the apparently even more domestic tides—"home" is repeated twice to describe the Bay of Fundy's ebb and flow. I say "apparently" because those tidal movements, though familiar to the speaker, suggest change and restlessness as much as recurrence. The speaker's eye moves downward from the daily human practices upon the land, to the water in its daily changes, to the mud beneath it with its "rivulets of fire." Her vision interweaves images of flux with images of continuity. If there is harmony in the landscape between the human and nonhuman elements— implicit in the attribution of human qualities to natural events ("home of the long tides," "the bay not at home"), and natural qualities to human artifacts (the red mud becoming the "red, gravelly roads" on which the bus is moving, and the churches described as "bleached, ridged as clamshells")—that harmony is at the same time qualified by the pervasive sense of temporal change, erosion, and decay inscribed in the very place itself. Even the homey comfortable enclosure of the bus, waiting "patient, while / a lone traveller gives / kisses and embraces / to seven relatives," is "beat-up" and "dented."

In the middle stanzas, as the bus journeys farther from home, the foggy evening, "shifting, salty, thin," heightens the speaker's feeling of dislocation. Like the method of imagism, the fog sharpens her perception of isolated objects by dissociating them from their familiar settings as well as from each other:

> Its cold, round crystals
> form and slide and settle
> in the white hens' feathers,
> in gray glazed cabbages,
> on the cabbage roses
> and lupins like apostles;
> . . . .
> A pale flickering. Gone.
> The Tantramar marshes
> and the smell of salt hay.
> An iron bridge trembles

and a loose plank rattles
but doesn't give way.

On the left, a red light
swims through the dark:
a ship's port lantern.
Two rubber boots show,
illuminated, solemn.
A dog gives one bark.

The dreamlike clarity of the details is in part a function of the undifferentiated background out of which they momentarily flash. If they retain a narrative aura, they pass and succeed each other too quickly to bestow on the speaker anything more than fragments of sense-impression. The speaker may sense some larger meaning in the boots that "show, / illuminated, solemn," but she passes by too quickly to identify that meaning. Like the poem in MacLeish's "Ars Poetica," each object does not mean but merely is. As they flare and vanish, these images specify the obliviating ground of change, which in the opening stanzas qualifies and is qualified in turn by the perception of the familiar and continuous. Now that home is behind her, though, the speaker sees the phenomenal world only in terms of an ever-vanishing present.

A woman climbs in
with two market bags,
brisk, freckled, elderly.
"A grand night. Yes, sir,
all the way to Boston."
She regards us amicably.
. . . .
The passengers lie back.
Snores. Some long sighs.
A dreamy divagation
begins in the night,
a gentle, auditory,
slow, hallucination. . . .

In the creakings and noises,
an old conversation

—not concerning us,
but recognizable, somewhere,
back in the bus:
Grandparents' voices

uninterruptedly
talking, in Eternity:
names being mentioned,
things cleared up finally;
what he said, what she said,
who got pensioned;

deaths, deaths and sicknesses;
the year he remarried;
the year (something) happened.
She died in childbirth.
That was the son lost
when the schooner foundered.

Though the stories "not concerning us" are also fragments, they are nonetheless so recognizable as "Grandparents' voices" that by implication they transport the speaker back to childhood. Against the relentlessly deracinating temporal current, they talk "uninterruptedly . . . in Eternity." And yet in the same way that the opening description of home combines images of change and persistence, these stories which return the speaker to the place she has left have to do with deaths and losses. In a sense the kind of storytelling enacted here is the way local cultures police their borders. Storytelling attempts to bind unpredictable catastrophes ("the year the schooner foundered") and inexplicable illnesses ("When Amos began to pray / . . . the family had / to put him away") in shared structures of meaning that may make it possible to go on living. What destroys life is made over, in the communal act of telling stories, into equipment for surviving and accepting that destruction:

"Yes . . . " that peculiar
affirmative. "Yes . . . "
A sharp, indrawn breath,
half groan, half acceptance,
that means "Life's like that.

> We know *it* (also death)."

> Talking the way they talked
> in the old featherbed,
> peacefully, on and on,
> dim lamplight in the hall,
> down in the kitchen, the dog
> tucked in her shawl.

Stories flow into the vacuum created by our losses, making acknowl-edgment of loss and imaginative restitution indivisible conditions of each other.

And yet, now that things have been "cleared up finally" and the voices cease ("Now, it's all right now / even to fall asleep / just as on all those nights"), the bus stops when a moose comes "out of / the impen-etrable wood," and everyone is jolted awake into a new attentiveness:

> Towering, antlerless,
> high as a church,
> homely as a house
> (or, safe as houses).
> A man's voice assures us
> "Perfectly harmless . . . "

> Some of the passengers
> exclaim in whispers,
> childishly, softly,
> "Sure are big creatures."
> "It's awful plain."
> "Look! It's a she!"

> Taking her time,
> she looks the bus over,
> grand, otherworldly.
> Why, why do we feel
> (we all feel) this sweet
> sensation of joy?

The moose incarnates the unpredictable which up to now has taken mostly catastrophic forms in the stories that the speaker overhears. If life surprises us with sorrow, it can surprise too with joy, which happily prevents the stories that we tell from clearing things up in any final or absolute way. The stories console and unify the people on the bus by addressing strictly human matters, whereas this encounter with the moose brings everyone into a community of joy that embraces more than the human, moving beyond the bus to include the natural world around it. In this light it is possible to see the bus as a symbol of human consciousness, "dented . . . beat up," bearing the marks of its temporal journey, yet open to the new and surprising, enclosed but not cut off from the mysteries of nature. Like the dog "tucked in her shawl," the moose is a feminine presence, "plain," "safe as houses," but also "otherworldly," "high as a church." The moose, too, is a natural version of the woman whose entrance in the bus initiates the storytelling. The adjective "grand" in relation to the moose echoes the woman's colloquial expression, "A grand night," linking the two, as if the moose's appearance were answering the woman's "amiable" openness to the night and its foggy mysteries. In combining the domestic and the strange, the moose embodies Bishop's vision of the sublime, not as an estranging presence but as something which despite or maybe even because of its difference nurtures a sense of mysterious kinship. But this encounter is only a moment in a longer journey and is quickly absorbed into the past, becoming one more story in a life of stories as the bus continues and "a dim / smell of moose" gives way to "an acrid / smell of gasoline."

5

In *Habits of the Heart: Individualism and Commitment in American Life* (Berkeley: University of California Press, 1985), Robert Bellah characterizes the bureaucratic corporate structure of American society as a culture of separation which has fostered the belief in a radically unencumbered and autonomous self:

> The most distinctive aspect of twentieth-century American society is the division of life into a number of separate functional sectors: home and workplace, work and leisure, white collar and blue collar, public and private. This division suited the needs of the

bureaucratic industrial corporations that provided the model for our preferred means of organizing society by the balancing and linking of sectors as "departments" in a functional whole, as in a great business enterprise.

If the sectoral structure of contemporary life has helped create a society that is "vastly more interrelated and integrated economically, technically and functionally," it has also made it increasingly difficult for the individual to "understand himself and his activities as interrelated in morally meaningful ways with those of other, different Americans." "Instead of directing cultural and individual energies toward relating the self to its larger context," the culture of separation "urges a strenuous effort to make of our particular segment of life a small world of its own." The separation of a public sphere of competition and professional advancement from a private sphere of leisure and consumption is also reflected in the separation of intellectual activity into specialized autonomous disciplines, each with its own mode of inquiry, its own set of problems, its own ends abstracted from the ends of other disciplines as well as from the broader questions of moral or social consequences.

Not surprisingly, this specializing tendency had been as evident in the arts as in industry. If the majority of modernist poets have attempted to restrict poetry to a purely discontinuous flow of images and symbols, the majority of my contemporaries have devoted their attentions exclusively to the personal expression of private experience, making themselves, in effect, experts of sensibility, with the same narrowness of focus as the economist who views all social problems through a strictly quantitative lens of benefits and costs, or the behavioral scientist whose strictly physiological perspective enables him to purify human action of any psychological intention, or the doctor whose strictly biomechanical concerns enable him to say, "The operation was a success, though the patient died."

One of the more encouraging developments in the postmodern period is the desire on the part of many scholars and intellectuals to dissolve the disciplinary boundaries of their respective fields. This interdisciplinary impulse has led in many cases to the recognition that constructing or attempting to construct a more inclusive knowledge of experience involves not just using the insights of other disciplines but forming those insights into a narrative that can relate the present to the past in useful and illuminating ways. In the appendix to *Habits of the Heart*, for instance, Bellah argues for a new kind of social science concerned with the whole of society, one that would integrate a sense of history with the specialized methods of empirical research. What that historical sense would supply, he says, is not merely information about the past, "but some idea of how we have gotten from the past to the present, in short, a narrative. Narrative is a primary and powerful way by which to know about a whole."

Scholars, intellectuals, and professionals in other fields are also drawing on narrative as a way of linking their specialized pursuits to the general culture. In *After Virtue* (Notre Dame: University of Notre Dame Press, 1984), Alasdair MacIntyre argues that every moral philosophy has some particular sociology as its counterpart; insofar as moral concepts are socially embedded in particular traditions, and in practices which in turn have particular histories, we cannot understand those concepts apart from the story or narrative of the culture that creates them: "We are, whether we acknowledge it or not, what the past has made us, and cannot eradicate from ourselves, even in America, those parts of ourselves which are formed by our relationship to each formative stage of our history." Even in the field of medicine, there are signs of growing impatience with the purely mechanical understanding of disease and treatment, dissociated from a patient's life history. In *The Illness Narratives* (New York: Basic Books, 1988), Dr. Arthur Kleinman demonstrates how the stories that patients tell about their chronic illnesses contribute "to the experience of symptoms and suffering." "The illness narrative," he says, "is a story the patient tells, and significant others retell, to give coherence to the distinctive events and long-term course of suffering. The plot lines, core metaphors, and rhetorical devices that structure the illness narratives are drawn from cultural and personal models for arranging experiences in meaningful ways and for effectively communicating those meanings." To the extent that these stories shape and create experience over the long course of a chronic illness, the doctor must make the empathic interpretation of those stories an important feature of his clinical care. One finds the same desire to relate biomedical dysfunctions to the whole of a patient's character in the work Oliver Sacks has done with patients suffering from neurological disorders such as postencephalitic Parkinsonism and Tourette's syndrome (see *Awakenings* [Garden City, NY: Doubleday, 1974] and *The Man Who Mistook His Wife for a Hat* [New York: Summit Books,

1985]). Like Kleinman, Sacks uses storytelling as a way of practicing what he calls a "romantic biology," the recognition of the indivisibility of body, character, and history. In *Awakenings* especially, he demonstrates how his patients' responses to chemotherapy are conditioned as much by their sense of being in the world, by the quality of their relationships and attitudes, as by their physiological makeup. One cannot therefore fully understand the course of an illness apart from the course of a life history.

The resuscitation of narrative by poets and artists in general parallels this emerging spirit of narrative in the general culture. It represents a serious rethinking of the particularly American belief in the autonomy of the individual and of the culture of separation which has fostered that belief. If much of our recent poetry can be characterized as the presentation of isolated "moments" of individual perception, poets such as C. K. Williams, Frank Bidart, Robert Pinsky, W. S. Di Piero, James McMichael, Ann Winters, and Eleanor Wilner (and many others) are recognizing that those "moments" are part of a transpersonal historical continuum which gives them their particular resonance and shape.

Narrative arises with the recognition that we are bearers of history. To see ourselves as embedded in the various traditions we inherit and transform, individually and collectively, in the course of living is to see life as a series of intersecting stories in which the self is simultaneously authored and authoring. As Alasdair MacIntyre remarks, "We enter a stage which we did not design, and we find ourselves part of an action that was not of our making. Each of us being a main character in his own drama plays subordinate parts in the drama of others, and each drama constrains the others." "Those Winter Sundays" and "Combat" illustrate the extent to which, in MacIntyre's words again, "the narrative of any one life is part of an interlocking set of narratives." The personal drama they enact is made intelligible only in relation to the drama of other lives as well as to the social and cultural stage on which those lives are acted, a stage which is, in turn, an effect of all the stories which precede and circumscribe each speaker's sense of who he is.

Again, this does not mean that the stories we tell are ever incontestable or absolutely true. As C. K. Williams reminds us in "Combat," our knowledge of who we are and where we come from is provisional at best. The legacies we inherit are too multifaceted ever to be completely comprehended, and the unanticipated ways in which our lives evolve change our perception of those legacies and the uses to which we put them. The responsible stories, the most inclusive ones, are those that acknowledge on some level their own incompleteness.

We are of course the bearers of more than social history. Our biological history joins us to the history of the living creatures on the planet. If our distinction as conscious creatures estranges us from that history, it also makes it possible for us to be aware of it, to see the human story relation to that larger story out of which the human comes. As Simone Weil observes, "every separation is a link." It is this paradoxical relation to the natural world that Bishop dramatizes in "The Moose." The human travelers see the moose as an amiable yet alien emissary from the impenetrable wood of their own preconscious nature. The medium that separates them from that mysterious source enables them to see and feel a kinship with it. In "By the Road to the Contagious Hospital," William Carlos Williams attempts to bridge the chasm between the human and natural by linking implicitly the story of spring emerging out of winter to the story of form emerging out of formlessness, spirit out of earth. Mind awakens by simultaneously rising up into the differentiating light and gripping down into the nurturing instinctive ground. Narrative impels the self outward not just to the social ecology of which it is a part, but also to the natural ecology which sustains it, from which it has arisen, and into which it will dissolve.

Perhaps what we ultimately acknowledge when we tell each other stories is that we are hostages to time. Becoming conscious creatures means exchanging stories about experience for mere participation in the experiential stream. Even if our stories dramatize the hope of stopping time, of preserving the ever-vanishing present, as acts of consciousness they only widen the separation they are meant to overcome: the more vividly a story brings the past into the present, the more acutely we experience the past as past. In a sense, narrative is the figure inscribed upon the ground of being, marking our provisional position as individuals and cultures in relation to unknown origins and unknown, unknowable ends. Stories are the elegiac gifts of human consciousness.

1990

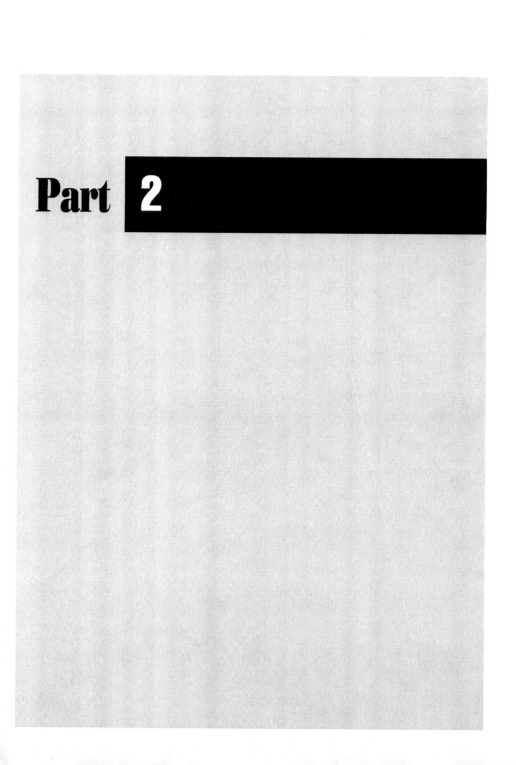

Part 2

The New Formalism

In the late sixties and early seventies when poetry became for me a serious pursuit, free verse was by far the dominant form. The majority of my contemporaries, for good or ill, were the grateful and uncritical inheritors of the most recent revolt against rhyme and meter which the previous generation of poets had initiated in the late fifties. The assumptions which stood back of the experiments and innovations undertaken by poets such as Ginsberg, Lowell, Bly, Ashbery, and Plath (to name only a few of the important innovators) had become by the early seventies sacred pieties. Though free verse did accommodate a diversity of styles, almost everyone who wrote free verse assumed that meter was an antiquated convention, artificial and repressive, and that free verse in all its various avatars alone permitted emotional and psychological authenticity, immediacy, and fidelity to contemporary speech.

In the mid-eighties, however, an opposite movement seems to be taking place. Open the pages of almost any national journal or magazine, and where ten years ago one found only one or another kind of free verse lyric, one now finds well-rhymed quatrains, sestinas, villanelles, sonnets, and blank verse dramatic monologues or meditations.[1] In a recent issue of *The New Criterion*, Robert Richman describes this rekindled interest in formal verse among younger poets as a "return to the high seriousness, eloquence and technical fluency" that characterized the best achievements of American poetry forty years ago.[2] As Mr. Richman numbers me among the younger poets now working in form, I ought to be as cheered by these developments as he is. Yet I am anything but cheered. And not because I don't want to belong to a club that would have me as a member, though this may be a part of it; but because I suspect that what Mr. Richman hails as a development may in fact be nothing but a mechanical reaction, and that the new formalists, in rejecting the sins of their experimental fathers may end up merely repeating the sins of their New Critical grandfathers, resuscitating the stodgy, over-refined conventions of the "fifties poem," conventions which were of course sufficiently narrow and restrictive to provoke rebellion in the first place. Any reform, carried to uncritical extremes by lesser talents who ignore rather than try to assimilate the achievements of their predecessors, will itself require reformation. If James Wright, say, or Robert Bly produced more than their fair share of imitators, if they even imitate themselves much of the time, they nonetheless have written poems all of us can and ought to learn from. Maybe we have had too much of the "raw" in recent years. But the answer to the raw is not the over-cooked. Besides, it's dangerous to think we have to choose exclusive-ly between free verse and form. The wider the range of styles and forms that we avail ourselves of, the more enriched, more flexible and inclusive our expressive resources will be. It's as important for those who work in form to be familiar with the experiments and innovations of the last hundred years as it is for those who work in looser mea-sures to be familiar with traditional verse forms that go back beyond the twentieth century.

But there's another cause of the uneasiness I feel at finding tradi-tional verse suddenly in vogue. As with any literary movement that becomes a literary fashion, much of the work now done in the name of a "return to high seriousness" is exceedingly dull. Dull formal work, I suppose, is no worse than dull experimental work. Yet one legacy of the exclusive thinking that dominates the literary scene is that for the past twenty years there has not been an active and informed tradition of standard verse among poets or poetry readers. Hence, though meter may be fashionable at present, very few of those who work in meter or who want to praise it know what good metrical verse is. Most poets and critics (friends and foes alike of traditional form) treat meter and rhythm as though they were synonymous, as though the metrical identity of a line of iambic pentameter, say, were equivalent to its rhythmical identity. The metrical norm of iambic pentameter, however, is an abstraction, a theoretical construction—I am, I am, I am, I am, I am—but because no two syllables carry the same stress, that is, the same length and degree of emphasis, every line of actual pentameter verse will and ought to depart to some extent from the metrical norm. The stress among the unswatted and swatted, unac-cented and accented, syllables will constantly vary even as the metri-cal scheme itself remains the same. It's possible then to write scores of iambic pentameter lines with no two sounding quite the same, lines which are metrically identical but rhythmically unique.

"The Heron," by Theodore Roethke, illustrates this distinction.

> The heron stands in water where the swamp
> Has deepened to the blackness of a pool,
> Or balances with one leg on a hump
> Of marsh grass heaped above a musk-rat hole.
>
> He walks the shallow with an antic grace.
> The great feet break the ridges of the sand,
> The long eye notes the minnow's hiding place,
> His beak is quicker than a human hand.
>
> He jerks a frog across his bony lip,
> Then points his heavy bill above the wood.
> The wide wings flap but once to lift him up.
> A single ripple starts from where he stood.[3]

The first line approaches the metrical norm more closely than any other line in the poem with the possible exception of the last line. The accented syllables are all heavily stressed to roughly the same degree and the unaccented syllables are lightly stressed to roughly the same degree. If one described the relative values of stress within the line numerically, the line would be 2,4/2,4/2,4/2,4/2,4. But compare this line with line eleven:

> The wide wings flap but once to lift him up
>   x   x   x   x   x   x

Here there are six heavily stressed syllables as a result of the heavily stressed foot in the second position ("wings flap"). To my ear, though "wings" is unaccented, receiving less stress than "flap," it actually carries more stress than the accented syllable of the first foot, "wide," creating in effect four degrees of rising emphasis in the first two feet. This together with the alliteration slows the verse down so that the rhythm implicates the slow yet powerful motion of the heron's wings. The line contains five iambic feet, but six heavily stressed syllables.

Line eight, on the other hand, contains only four heavy stresses:

> His beak is quicker than a human hand
>   x   x   x   x

The more lightly stressed contour of the line is consistent with the sudden quickness of the heron's beak darting for the minnow. Our perception of the quickening and slowing down of the line is made possible by our simultaneous perception of the metrical norm and the subtle variations of stress which modulate it. Again, all these lines are metrically identical. They all contain five iambic feet, but the amount of stress within each iambic foot is continually varied, the stresses changing as the objects of Roethke's attention change. Rhythm, of course, is more than the variations of stress within a metrical scheme. Syntax in relation to line and stanza, substitution of one kind of foot for another, punctuation, pitch, and volume all influence the rhythmical life of a poem. It's a measure of Roethke's skill and of the expressive potentialities of the iambic line that he enjambs so little, endstops every quatrain, never substitutes at all, and still avoids monotony.

"The Heron," however, is a simple, unambitious poem, its simplicity reflected stylistically in the purely descriptive language and uncomplicated syntax, and technically in the coincidence of the syntactical units with the line and quatrain. "Church Monuments," by George Herbert, is a much more complex poem emotionally and intellectually, and this complexity has consequences for the handling of the form.

> While that my soul repairs to her devotion,
> Here I entomb my flesh, that it betimes
> May take acquaintance of this heap of dust;
> To which the blast of death's incessant motion,
> Fed with the exhalation of our crimes,
> Drives all at last. Therefore I gladly trust
>
> My body to this school, that it may learn
> To spell his elements, and find his birth
> Written in dusty heraldry and lines;
> Which dissolution sure doth best discern,
> Comparing dust with dust, and earth with earth.
> These laugh at jet, and marble put for signs,
>
> To sever the good fellowship of dust,
> And spoil the meeting. What shall point out them,
> When they shall bow, and kneel, and fall down flat

> To kiss those heaps, which now they have in trust?
> Dear flesh, while I do pray, learn here thy stem
> And true descent, that when thou shalt grow fat
>
> And wanton in thy cravings, thou mayst know
> That flesh is but the glass which holds the dust
> That measures all our time; which also shall
> Be crumbled into dust. Mark, here below
> How tame these ashes are, how free from lust,
> That thou mayst fit thyself against thy fall.[4]

The poem is a meditation on death, on the instabilities within apparent permanence. While his soul repairs to her devotions, the speaker meditates before the tombs, "Comparing dust with dust, and earth with earth," in hope that the flesh—the appetites and desires which tie him to the physical world, to sin and death—will learn that the only genuine stability derives from Christian Grace. The church monuments, ordinarily symbolic of familial continuity, here become symbolic of ultimate decay since they themselves are crumbling along with the ashes they entomb. Only in dissolution will the flesh discern its true lineage, its "true descent" (in both senses of the word), "written in dusty heraldry and lines":

> Dear flesh, while I do pray, learn here thy stem
> And true descent, that when thou shalt grow fat
>
> And wanton in thy cravings, thou mayst know
> That flesh is but the glass which holds the dust
> That measures all our time; which also shall
> Be crumbled into dust. Mark, here below
> How tame these ashes are, how free from lust,
> That thou mayst fit thyself against thy fall.

Notice that the first four lines of the last stanza are all enjambed, and that the enjambments create two pentameter units: the unit of the line itself ("And wanton in thy cravings, thou mayst know"), and a second pentameter unit cutting across the lines from caesura to caesura ("thou mayst know that flesh is but the glass" "which holds the dust that measures all our time" "which also shall be crumbled into dust"). This effect is coincident with the figure of the hourglass which, like the monuments, is crumbling along with the dust that it contains. If the stanzaic structure is analogous to the apparent stability of the glass and of "the jet and marble" of the tombs, the syntactical movement corresponds in turn to the forces of impermanence and change at work within all earthly things. Herbert creates an illusion of instability through the longer clauses drawn across the lines, accelerating the movement of the verse without at the same time destroying the illusion of stability which the lines and stanzas generate. The enjambments are not so radical that the line, that first-parameter measure, ceases to be heard. And yet the enjambments are all the more effective, seem more radical than they in fact are, because the lines preceding them are relatively endstopped.

Without some sort of discernible recurrence of sound and structure, some norm of expectation, no surprise, no significant variation is possible. And the more clearly articulated a metrical scheme is, the more firmly it entrenches a habit of expectation, the more surprising and unexpected and potentially expressive will be the slightest alteration. If there's too much regularity and not enough subtle pressure of stress against the metrical norm, we have meter without rhythm. The verse degenerates into a singsong mechanical monotony. If there's too much variation, on the other hand, we have only another kind of monotony, for the variations, no longer in tension with a metrical norm, are no longer varying from anything. Just as some Information theorists regard "news" as inversely proportioned to its expectedness—the entirely expected is never news—so in metrical composition, repetition and surprise, the anticipated and unanticipated, are interdependent.[5] To surprise is to upset an expectation. And the deeper the expectation, the greater the potential surprise.

This sort of rhythmical control is precisely what I find lacking in so much of the formal verse now being written. Most of the new formalists either adhere too predictably to the metrical grid or depart too violently from it. And both extremes often appear together in the same poem. Take, for example, "Learning to Whistle," a poem by Norman Williams, one of the poets whom Richman praises for his technical sophistication. "Learning to Whistle" is from Williams' new book, *The Unlovely Child*, recently published by Knopf.

> At once, the breath, the lips, the tongue:
> Something which, or said my father,

As he larked it in garage and cellar,
Could not be taught but had to be
Discovered, each man for himself,
And so, just four, I bundled in
A kitchen corner, before anyone
Was up, and in the church-weak light
Of winter, blew until light-headed.
For lisping months I carried on,
Until, one day taking me aside,
My mother told me in her house
One whistler was enough. But now
I have reached my father's age
And, astonished, find myself
With his odd eye and thinning hair—
At times, too, I try once more
For what was then beyond my reach:
Mostly still the sibilants, but then,
Too, ever so occasionally, a tone.[6]

In some lines we have a stiff march of Frankensteinian iambs and trochees ("At once, the breath, the lips, the tongue: / Something which, or said my father"), in other lines nothing but lineated prose ("A kitchen corner, before anyone / was up" "Until, one day taking me aside"). Likewise, in some places the syntax is idiomatic and casual, in other places, egregiously contorted to fit the four beat norm ("Something which, or said my father"). Now one could argue that this clumsiness is intentional, reflecting the child's first awkward unsuccessful attempts to imitate his father. Yet intentional clumsiness is still clumsiness. A more sensitive handling of meter could suggest the same strain without being strained itself (see line six of "The Heron"), and at the same time it could implicate other fine shades of feeling and perception. Williams conveys the small boy's awkwardness and a soupy wistfulness about the past (note the rather hackneyed poeticized description of whistling—"lisping" and "larking"), but little else. The crude management of form can render only crude overgeneralized emotions.

If "Learning to Whistle" shows how metrical unpredictability and rhythmical monotony go hand in hand, "Cruising with the Beach Boys," a poem by Dana Gioia which recently appeared in *Poetry* (and then won the Frederick Bock prize), errs in the opposite direction:

> So strange to hear that song again tonight
> Travelling on business in a rented car
> Miles from anywhere I've been before.
> And now a tune I haven't heard for years
> Probably not since it last left the charts
> Back in L.A. in 1969.
> I can't believe I know the words by heart
> And can't think of a girl to blame them on.
>
> Every lovesick summer has its song,
> And this one I pretended to despise,
> But if I were alone when it came on,
> I turned it up full-blast to sing along—
> A primal scream in croaky baritone,
> The notes all flat, the lyrics mostly slurred.
> No wonder I spent so much time alone
> Making the rounds in Dad's old Thunderbird.
>
> Some nights I drove down to the beach to park
> And walk along the railings of the pier.
> The water down below was cold and dark,
> The waves monotonous against the shore.
> The darkness and the mist, the midnight sea,
> The flickering lights reflected from the city—
> A perfect setting for a boy like me,
> The Cecil B. DeMille of my self-pity.
>
> I thought by now I'd left those nights behind,
> Lost like the girls that I could never get,
> Gone with the years, junked with the old T-Bird.
> But one old song, a stretch of empty road,
> Can open up a door and let them fall
> Tumbling like boxes from a dusty shelf,
> Tightening my throat for no reason at all
> Bringing on tears shed only for myself.[7]

Technically, this is unobjectionable. The meter is handled smoothly, the sentences are all drawn naturally through the lines and stanzas with little straining after rhyme, and the style overall is unforced and idiomatic, in keeping with the ordinariness of the occasion. Yet if the metrical frame doesn't interfere with what the poet has to say, it doesn't respond to, or animate, it either. The bland, mildly humorous diction drones on with the cadence, as though on automatic pilot. It drones on, moreover, even in the few places where the metrical norm is ruffled. In the last stanza, for instance, Gioia brings three trochaic substitutions together in the space of two lines:

> I thought by now I'd left those nights behind,
> Lost like the girls that I could never get,
> Gone with the years, junked with the old T-Bird.

The slight metrical disruption is intended to intensify the somewhat embarrassed, somewhat melancholy realization that his sentimental longings have persisted. Yet notice the participles the trochaic substitutions make emphatic: "lost," "gone," and "junked." In context, these are not only utterly predictable, they are also of a piece with the blasé language of the rest of the poem. They in no way justify or support the attention which the metrical change arouses.

But there's a more important point to be made about both poems. The slack rhythms of each reflect an overall slackness and complacency of language and detail; they belie a slackness of attention to the realities the poets are attempting to evoke. In "Learning to Whistle," for instance, the father's "odd eye and thinning hair," which the speaker discovers emerging in his own appearance, tell us precious little about the father, or about the father/son relationship, or the legacy the son inherits from the father beyond a pat external likeness. Hence the astonishment he lays claim to is a sentimental overstatement, and the tone he "ever occasionally" achieves—because it does not issue from a persuasively delineated context—carries no specific weight or meaning. "Cruising with the Beach Boys" is similarly vague and stereotypical. Again, one could argue that the stale description in the second stanza of the speaker's nighttime walks along the ocean provides an implicit commentary on the sentimentality which drew him there, and which the song renews. One could even regard the trite language as a measure of the poet's restraint, his tactful unwillingness to make more of this experience than it deserves. But instead of attempting to insinuate such a complex attitude into the language, so that the scene itself embodies both the self-indulgence and the struggle to restrain it (think in this connection of Lawrence's "Piano"), Gioia offers us the stale props of adolescent longing over several lines, which he then undercuts at the end of the stanza with an equally stale punch line, "The Cecil B. DeMille of my self-pity." The apparent self-deprecation masks a certain smugness: "Aren't I wonderful," he tells us, "for knowing how foolishly sentimental I once was."

The restraint reflected in the low-key style and metrical stringencies of each poem are nowhere strained against, or challenged and made necessary by any emotional or psychological counterstress, any intensity of mind. It's as though both poets believed that the erection of a metrical frame around a subject was all the imaginative work they had to do. But as Coleridge reminds us in his illuminating discussion of meter in the *Biographia Literaria*, the formal aspects of a poem have no value apart from the intense attentiveness they help to dramatize.[8] Coleridge's theory of meter is inextricably bound up with his theory of imagination, of that power of consciousness which "reveals itself in the balance and reconciliation of opposite and discordant qualities, of sameness with difference; of the general with the concrete, the idea with the image . . . the sense of novelty and freshness with the old and familiar objects; a more than usual state of order with a more than usual state of feeling. . . . " If the best poetry provides a model of consciousness at its most inclusive and active, then the formal tensions, the rhythmical interplay of stress and accent, sentence and line, become the technical extension or expression of the imagination's power to unify and balance. We can think of meter as analogous to the familiar, the expected, the more than usual state of order; and the variety of rhythmical effects as corresponding to the concrete, the sense of novelty and freshness and a more than usual state of feeling. In its active engagement with a subject, meter provides a kind of dynamic restraint. In much the same way that the narrow banks of a channel can intensify a flow of water, meter can hold in check the workings of passion at the same time as it speeds them on. But to restrain in this way implies the presence of some powerful energy in need of restraining. To arouse and heighten expectation and attention through the subtle recurrences and variations of sound implies something in the subject worth expecting and attending to. Meter in and of itself is worthless. Its value is contingent on the value of the matter it expresses and reveals. When such corresponding substance is lacking, when the technique is crudely or mechanically related to the theme, we feel a disappointment, "like that of leaping in the dark from the last step of a staircase, when we had prepared our muscles for a leap of three or four."[9]

We feel no such disappointment in Timothy Dekin's poem "Sunday Visiting Day." The poem, in iambic pentameter couplets, forms the penultimate section of a sequence depicting the breakup of a marriage. Separated from his wife, the speaker pays a visit to his young son:

> Your room's no different, but some toys are new.
> We kiss. I wonder who gave them to you,
> But don't ask. You are almost talking now,
> Something I can't quite get about a cow,
> A secret conversation you and she
> Share, laughing, while I eavesdrop bitterly.
> I hug you, gorging myself on the taste,
> Touch, smell of you who shrug me off in haste
> To play again: you've seen the bright red car
> Your friend is holding, playing in the yard.
> Your clear face breaking into tears, you run
> Shouting Mine, mine mine! Like father like son.[10]

Line by line, couplet by couplet, the poem enacts a kind of psychological drama in which the speaker struggles with less and less success to hold in check the turbulent emotions he feels now in the presence of the family he no longer has. Notice that the cadence of the second line is somewhat ambiguous; it moves precariously from anapestic tetrameter to the pentameter norm. If we let the norm resolve this ambiguity of emphasis, we're forced to promote the stress on "who" and "them," bringing into sharp relief the speaker's jealous fear that another man may have usurped his role as father and husband, a fear he no sooner expresses than he's compelled to stifle in the following line. The slightly roughened cadence of the enjambed phrase, "But don't ask," suggests not only the intensity of his fear, but also— because of this intensity—the necessity and difficulty of repressing it. His sense of exclusion grows even more acute in the third couplet, the first place in the poem where the closure of sentence and line coincides. The linebreak after "you and she," and the heavily stressed first foot of the following line, "Share, laughing," point up the father's bitter perception of the intimacy which the mother and son now share, the rhyme itself reflecting the pain of his estrangement. And this in turn leads to the father's sudden release of feeling, to which the child responds by shrugging him off to run after the toy his friend is holding. What makes the end so moving is the way the child's grief over losing the bright red car embodies the father's grief over losing the child, and the ironic bond this establishes between them in the father's mind. The commonplace ("Like father like son"), trained on such an unexpected situation, has all the force and surprise of a discovery. The grief, which the child can innocently indulge, the father—in the interest of preserving a mature veneer—must struggle to keep hidden. It's this interior action which the rhythms help to dramatize, straining against but never quite breaking the metrical scheme.

Timothy Steele establishes an equally expressive, equally dramatic tension between form and content in "Profils Perdus," a poem about a kind of Jamesian impressionist, about someone so given over to sheer process, uninformed or shaped by the discriminating powers of the mind, that he is nothing but his own ephemeral sensations:

It does not matter if in Rome that fall
You, leaning on the rail of the balcony,
Watched a young woman pace the yard below,
Her parasol
Now raised, now shouldered. Nor need you feel, see,

More in the sudden rain which, in Marseilles,
Forced you into that church than the stained glass,
Or the four white candles, or the vast stillness,
Or the way
The marble echoes rippled through the Mass.

Nostalgia is your last, your perfect, fate.
In the vague wash of circumstance, you know
That any instant can in you assume
All the weight
And feeling of the absolute. And so,

What matters, simply, is that you contain
Both past and future; that sometime, somewhere,

> You will yourself become the moment—an
> Indefinite rain,
> A profile disappearing in the air.[11]

Since for this character only the sensation of the moment exists, and since the moment is, by definition, fugitive, "nostalgia is his last, his perfect fate." Without recourse to the past in the form of either memory, language, or social institutions, he can learn nothing from his experience, because experience, for him, is nothing but "a vague wash of circumstance." He contains both past and future, moreover, only in the sense that, since he cannot discriminate among the succession of moments that comprise his life, his life becomes completely uniform, nothing but a rain.

The irregular line lengths and the seemingly loose movement of the syntax from one line to the next give the illusion of freedom (note the linebreak after "an"), as if the dictates of the moment itself were governing the movement of the verse. And yet Steele achieves this effect by means of the strict elements of the form. It's the metrical pattern that gives point to the variations he plays across it, just as it's the fixed stanzaic structure that makes the formlessness, as formlessness, perceptible.

Because the expressive possibilities of form remain unused or crudely used in "Cruising with the Beach Boys and "Learning to Whistle," one can imagine any number of other forms (including prose) in which these subjects could be treated with just as much or little effectiveness. At best, the formal elements provide nothing but a badge of affiliation, a kind of aesthetic tattoo or Good Housekeeping seal—they distinguish these poems from the standard fare of free-verse lyrics, but they animate and reveal no particular insight or understanding. Which is to say that the formal elements do nothing but declare their own formality. If writing free verse, as Robert Frost maintains, is like playing tennis without the net, writing this sort of formal verse (and it's the sort most visible nowadays) is like playing tennis with the net but without the ball.

As I mentioned in the beginning of this essay, in the sixties and seventies one often heard the argument that meter and rhyme are emotionally and psychologically repressive, and that a preference for closed forms goes hand in hand with a preference for closed, authoritarian societies. To Robert Bly, for instance, metrical composition reflected a "nostalgia for jails."[12]   What our technology—the product of a hyperrational culture—was doing to the people of the third world our metrical techniques were doing to our own emotions, to our unconscious "rebellious energy," from which alone authentic art can spring. Likewise, Galway Kinnell assumed that anyone who wrote in meter automatically believed that "just as the highest virtues of the state are law and order, so the highest virtue in poetry is formality and morality."[13] It's no surprise, then, that in the eighties a return to formal poetry should be described as the aesthetic expression of the conservatism one finds everywhere throughout the culture, a kind of aesthetic Reaganomics. In an essay entitled "The Yuppie Poet," which appeared in a recent issue of the Associated Writing Programs newsletter, Ariel Dawson equates "the reemergence of formalism" with the "renewed interest in country clubs."[14] Ms. Dawson would doubtless argue that it's no accident that this rekindled interest in traditional verse would be hailed in the pages of *The New Criterion*. That artistic changes are influenced by social and political changes seems beyond dispute. What is not beyond dispute, however, is the rather simpleminded concept of influence and determinism implicit in this connection between political allegiance and aesthetic choice. If free-verse experimentation necessarily entailed allegiance to progressive thinking, what are we to make of Pound and Eliot, the great twentieth-century free-verse innovators, whose right-wing authoritarian politics make Reagan seem like a wishy-washy liberal.

The politicization of poetic form can just as easily be turned against those who argue that free verse is intrinsically open, organic, exploratory, natural, and faithful to the contours of contemporary experience, and that predetermined forms are intrinsically mechanical, calculating, artificial, and closed. Indeed, the cult of the moment, the fetishizing of the new and distrust of the old, is itself symptomatic of our consumer culture, of an economy reared on the principle of planned obsolescence, on the obliteration of the customary and habitual in the name of endless growth, in the name of new and larger markets which require the constant and artificial stimulation of new and larger appetites. To be a child of one's time, as Wendell Berry points out, at this time is to be a child of a world in which fads and fashions have displaced all sense of durable value, which is to say, a world created by merchandisers.[15] Pound's rallying cry, "Make it new," is, now, also Madison Avenue's. And whereas Madison Avenue continues to make it new at a bewildering speed, as the late J. V. Cunningham once observed, our poets have been making it new in the same old ways for over seventy years. This esteem for the present, moreover, has been institutionalized in the majority of MFA writing programs across the country in which very little training in the literary past is required. Because each new generation of poets must devise its own forms in order to express its own unique moment of experience, they assume that poetry from Homer to the present century (because in meter) has nothing to teach them. Hence Eliot's sense of the past, which he believed indispensable to anyone who would continue writing poetry beyond his twenty-fifth year, has become a thing of the past. Yet the value of tradition, of writing with "a feeling that the whole of the literature of Europe from Homer and within it the whole of the literature of his own country has a simultaneous existence and composes a simultaneous order," is precisely the long view that provides a larger context of experience within which, and by means of which, we may better discriminate irrelevant from relevant, necessary from unnecessary, values, concerns, and practices. Without a living sense of the past, we can only be a prey to fashion.

It would be encouraging to think that more and more poets are drawn to formal verse out of an impatience with the narrow and ossified conventions of so much recent poetry, with the mannered nakedness that passes for free verse. But metrical composition will itself turn out to be just one more passing fad if those who practice it don't give themselves a thorough grounding in the prosodic past and acquire an instinctive sense of the delicate and subtle tensions between stress and accent, rhythm and meter, repetition and surprise, which the best poems in the tradition illustrate. I have been moved to write this essay because the formal work now receiving the most attention, work such as "Learning to Whistle" and "Cruising with the Beach Boys," does reinforce the stereotype that metrical verse is stilted and mechanical. And insofar as it does this, it perpetuates the false dichotomies which have enforced false choices, choices which are false because exclusive. As I hope my discussion of "Sunday Visiting Day" and "Profils Perdus" have shown, not only can one write with feeling, honesty, and naturalness in traditional measures, in strict forms, but also the very formal complexity such strictness generates makes possible a complex and detailed rendering of experience. These poems realize the classical ideal of integrating the oldest of the new with the newest of the old; they are traditional and fresh, intelligent and full of passion. They dramatize not "a nostalgia for jails," but a desire to bring the widest, most unrestricted play of mind and heart to bear upon the widest range of life.

1986

Notes

1. There is an abundant evidence for this rekindled interest in formal poetry. To cite just a few examples, this year (1986), Harper and Row has published an anthology called *Strong Measures* devoted exclusively to traditional verse. The anthology, so the blurb on the back cover informs us, "celebrates the renaissance of formal verse in contemporary America. As Richard Wilbur writes in his foreword, more and more poets have begun to realize that rhyme and meter are "not ornament but emphasis . . . " Vikram Seth's novel in tetrameter sonnets, *Golden Gate*, published this past January (1986), has become something of a sensation, receiving notices everywhere, including *Newsweek*, a magazine in which poetry is seldom reviewed. Even opponents of traditional poetry have recognized this "renaissance." See my comments on Ariel Dawson, below.

2. Robert Richman, "Poetry and the Return to Seriousness," *The New Criterion* (Summer 1985): 39.

3. Theodore Roethke, *Words for the Wind* (Indiana, 1970), 24.

4. George Herbert, *Selected Poems*, ed. Joseph Summers (New York, 1967), 106.

5. For an illuminating discussion of information theory and aesthetic form see E. H. Gombrich, "Expression and Communication," in *Meditations on a Hobby Horse* (London, 1978), 60.

6. Norman Williams, *The Unlovely Child* (New York, 1985), 15.

7. Dana Gioia, *Poetry* (August 1985): 263.

8. S. T. Coleridge, *Biographia Literaria*, ed. James Engell and W. J. Bate (Princeton, 1983), chap. 18: 60–73.

9. Ibid., chap. 18: 66.

10. Timothy Dekin, *Winter Fruit* (Chicago, 1982), 44.

11. Timothy Steele, *Uncertainties and Rest* (Baton Rouge, 1979), 5.

12. Robert Bly, *Naked Poetry*, ed. Robert Mezey and Stephen Berg (New York, 1969), 161–64.

13. Galway Kinnell, "Poetry, Personality, and Death," *Field* 4 (Spring 1971): 67.

14. Ariel Dawson, "The Yuppie Poet," *AWP Newsletter* (May 1985): 4.

15. Wendell Berry, "The Specialization of Poetry," *The Poet's Work*, ed. Reginald Gibbons (Boston, 1979), 148.

Some Notes on Free Verse and Meter

1. Poetic rhythm exists on a continuum between mere formal marching on the one hand, and mere movement on the other. Every actual poem, metered and unmetered alike, will fall somewhere between these abstract poles, and the segment it occupies will replicate them in miniature to one degree or another. In relation to Donne's *Satires*, the iambic pentameter of Sidney's "With How Sad Steps" lies closer to the hypermetrical end of the continuum, but in relation to George Gascoigne's "Woodmanship" it lies closer to the opposite, more "open" extreme. To an eighteenth-century reader whose ear had been trained by Dryden and Pope, Blake's "Ah Sunflower" would have probably sounded chaotic or incompetent; yet to an American reader whose ear has been trained by the prosodic experiments of Williams or Pound, the poem will sound closer to the metrical formalities that he or she, however crudely, associates with neoclassicism. Even among poems that lie near the other end of the spectrum, there will likewise be some sort of tension between fixity and flux, the random and repetitive, with some poems tending toward the one extreme, and some toward the other. Relative to the meters of Tennyson, Whitman's unmetered lines seem loosely organized. Yet relative to Williams' more colloquial idiom, syntactical diversity, and radical enjambments, his biblical oratory, reinforced by an unvaried coincidence of phrase and line, seems closer, within the range of what free verse can do, to the formal end of the spectrum. No matter where the poem falls on this continuum, its rhythmical life will still, in varying degrees, arise from and depend on an expressive interplay between the antithetical forces (in one form or another) of order and freedom, repetition and surprise, continuity and change, conformity to rule and individuation, familiarity and strangeness.

On the other hand, if the rhythmical effects of free verse and metrical verse differ only in degree, the differences are real. Metered and unmetered verse begin from opposite ends of the spectrum, and in the poetry I find most interesting often move in opposite directions. The poet writing in meter begins in restraint and moves toward freedom, or rather tests the possibilities of freedom within the limitations of a given form, while the poet writing in free verse begins in freedom and solicits from it nonnumerical possibilities of order. To adapt Eliot's formulation, if the ghost of some simple meter should lurk behind the arras of even the freest verse, the ghost of freedom should haunt even the most articulated measure.

2. Because it takes what Pound called "the variable element" or change as its norm, and since change is a condition of novelty, and of astonishment (the emotional consequence or effect of novelty), free verse naturally lends itself in its most radical forms to the random flash, the evanescent, the momentary. It appeals to our desire as creatures of sense to live forever in a world of fresh perception. At the same time, we desire more than this. As historical and social beings, we desire structures of thought and action that extend beyond the moment so as to help us organize and control our lives. That is, we desire continuity as much as we do the intensities which fresh perception generates, intensities which can only be sustained by constant dislocation. Thus what we experience (from the vantage point of one desire) as liberation from the deadening weight of custom we experience (in terms of other needs and appetites) as deracination.

3. Imagism, one could argue, represented an attempt to engage both desires. It expanded the subject matter of early twentieth-century American poetry by turning away from the outworn, overly rarefied conventions of late Victorian romanticism in the interests of quotidian reality—people in a metro station, jazz, motor cars, urban decay, etc. Just as it embraced contemporary life, it cultivated a more contemporary idiom. The imagists rejected the poetic diction of their predecessors, what Pound called the "doughy mess of third-hand Keats, Wordsworth, Elizabethan sonority, blunted, half-melted, lumpy," in favor of the language as it was actually spoken. And Imagism also introduced a degree of concrete sensory experience seldom found in any poetry written before the present century. On the other hand, in its general distrust of convention or discursiveness of any kind, in its exclusive devotion to juxtaposing images, imagism had the contrary effect of intensifying poetic language by reducing its range and, as a consequence of this intensity, of isolating the poem from ordinary experience and from other forms of discourse. Imagism was a short-lived movement because in its purest form it could foster only fragments, isolated flashes of perception. It could not accommodate the more inclusive world of social and political realities, the world of choice, action, commitment and discovery within which much of our lives takes place. While H. D., Pound, and Williams felt confined by imagism even as they perfected it, still in their longer poems they relied primarily on imagist techniques to organize the material they were bringing together. One wonders if the preoccupation in the modern epic with brokenness and isolation doesn't have as much to do with these aesthetic biases as with any sense of cultural crisis and the breakdown of communal order. The desire for order and coherence may be implicit in the longer, more inclusive structures of the *Cantos*, *Paterson*, or *Helen in Egypt*, but the techniques that organize those poems, being primarily techniques of dissociation, could only frustrate that desire.

4. On the other hand, imagism was an indispensable stage in the development of a free verse that could appeal both to our hunger for intensity of sense perception and to our need for organizing structure. We find in the best poems by Williams, Pound, Eliot, Mina Loy, Basil Bunting, or Wallace Stevens, as well as in the free verse of more recent writers such as Lowell, Bishop, Wright, and many others, a free verse that attempts in different ways to find nonmetrical equivalents for metrical effects, so that without abandoning intellectual control or judgment (the capacity to connect one moment with another), it can stay as close as possible to its experiential and linguistic sources, to the language as it's actually spoken on the one hand, and to the open and fluid textures of lived experience on the other. Which is to say that in place of the control afforded by a strict metrical pattern, free verse relies on structural elements common to all linguistic acts, that is, it doesn't superimpose an additional or secondary convention upon the language (beyond the convention of lineation) but attempts to establish its formal shape from within the language itself. In such verse syntax becomes an indispensable source of prosodic expectation and surprise both within and across the lines.

The power of Whitman's poetry derives in part from the complicated relation of syntax to rhythm: the open paratactic sentences across the lines together with the ever-changing, nonrecurring movement of syllables within the lines, enhance his celebratory evocation of the natural freedom of the single solitary self ("Nature without check with original energy"); at the same time, the parallel clauses repeating the same grammatical structure down the page, as well as the same relation to the line, acknowledge, tacitly at least, a complementary commitment to a world shared with others, to communal life ("Through me many long dumb voices"). Taken all together, we have in effect a prosodic equivalent to his democratic dream of unity within multiplicity, sameness within difference, individual freedom and social conscience.

5. We can better appreciate the different effects which free verse and metrical verse can generate by looking at two poems, "The Slow Pacific Swell" by Yvor Winters and "The Cod Head" by William Carlos Williams, two poems which use antithetical forms to treat a similar occasion and a similiar theme. Both poems view the sea as a literal symbol of the separation of mind from the material universe, of human consciousness from the unconscious, random and corrosive energies within the self as well as in the world. Though both poems attempt to bring mind and sea into intimate relation, to open up the mind to its own brute, mindless ground of being, both at the same time recognize, directly or indirectly, that consciousness of nature means estrangement from nature, that the very ability to perceive, appreciate, and understand the beauty and power of the natural world depends on the very faculty which cuts us off from it. "The Slow Pacific Swell," however, is written in iambic pentameter couplets, whereas "The Cod Head" employs a sinewy, highly enjambed free verse line. These metrical differences reflect fundamental differences in tone and attitude, differences which undercut certain prevailing assumptions about the relation of open and closed forms to emotional intensity and intellectual judgment.

The Slow Pacific Swell

Far out of sight forever stands the sea,
Bounding the land with pale tranquillity.
When a small child, I watched it from a hill
At thirty miles or more. The vision still
Lies in the eye, soft blue and far away:
The rain has washed the dust from April day;
Paint-brush and lupine lie against the ground;
The wind above the hill-top has the sound
Of distant water in unbroken sky;
Dark and precise the little steamers ply—

Firm in direction they seem not to stir.
That is illusion. The artificer
Of quiet, distance holds me in a vise
And holds the ocean steady to my eyes.

Once when I rounded Flattery, the sea
Hove its loose weight like sand to tangle me
Upon the washing deck, to crush the hull;
Subsiding, dragged flesh at the bone. The skull
Felt the retreating wash of dreaming hair.
Half drenched in dissolution, I lay bare.
I scarcely pulled myself erect; I came
Back slowly, slowly knew myself the same.
That was the ocean. From the ship we saw
Gray whales for miles: the long sweep of the jaw,
The blunt head plunging clean above the wave.
And one rose in a tent of sea and gave
A darkening shudder; water fell away;
The whale stood shining, and then sank in spray.

A landsman, I. The sea is but a sound.
I would be near it on a sandy mound,
And hear the steady rushing of the deep
While I lay stinging in the sand with sleep.
I have lived inland long. The land is numb.
It stands beneath the feet, and one may come
Walking securely, till the sea extends
Its limber margin, and precision ends.
By night a chaos of commingling power,
The whole Pacific hovers hour by hour.
The slow Pacific swell stirs on the sand,
Sleeping to sink away, withdrawing land,
Heaving and wrinkled in the moon, and blind;
Or gathers seaward, ebbing out of mind.

The Cod Head

Miscellaneous weed
strands, stems, debris—
firmament

to fishes—
where the yellow feet
of gulls dabble

oars whip
ships churn to bubbles—
at night wildly

agitate phospores-
cent midges—but by day
flaccid

moons in whose
discs sometimes a red cross
lives—four

fathom—the bottom skids
a mottle of green
sands backward—

amorphous waver-
ing rocks—three fathom
the vitreous

body through which—
small scudding fish deep
down—and

now a lulling lift
and fall—
red stars—a severed cod-

head between two
green stones—lifting
falling

Insofar as both poems present a solitary speaker contemplating a nat-
ural scene, they continue the romantic tradition of the descriptive-
meditative lyric, the classic exemplars of which are Wordsworth's
"Tintern Abbey" and Coleridge's "Frost At Midnight." "The Slow

Pacific Swell," though, in overall design lies closer than "The Cod Head" to its romantic predecessors, not only because it's much more personal, more intensely emotive, mixing recollection, description, and meditation, but also because it follows almost to the letter the tripartite structure M. H. Abrams claims is central to this kind of poem: like the speaker in "Tintern Abbey" or "Frost At Midnight," the speaker in "The Slow Pacific Swell" "begins with a description of the landscape; an aspect or change in the landscape evokes a varied but integral process of memory, thought, anticipation, and feeling which remains closely involved with the outer scene. In the course of this meditation the lyric speaker achieves an insight, faces up to a tragic loss, comes to a moral decision, or resolves an emotional problem. Often the poem rounds upon itself to end where it began, at the outer scene, but with an altered mood and deepened understanding which is the result of the intervening meditation."

As in the great romantic lyrics, there are two visions implicit in the description in the opening stanza: the Edenic vision of the natural world in which sea and land, water and sky, the small and delicate, and the vast and powerful, all nourish and sustain each other in pantheistic harmony, and the fallen or experienced vision of the adult who understands that what he sees and is still moved by ("The vision still / Lies in the eye soft blue and far away") is false and dangerously alluring. The former perspective of the child is limited to sense impression, to the eye's bodily delight in mere appearance, its intensity a function of its narrowness of range, while the latter perspective of the adult includes but goes beyond the sensory to judge and discriminate what the eye receives ("That is illusion"). The handling of the verse form reinforces the vision of a tidy and harmonious relation among the various elements in the scene: the couplets are mostly closed, and where there is some enjambment, the line cuts into the sentence at relatively stable places. The meter is likewise firmly established. Aside from the conventional use of trochaic substitution in the first foot of lines 2, 5, 10, 11, and 12, there is no disruption of the metrical pattern, and even the variation of stress among the accented and unaccented syllables is relatively slight. The two places in which enjambment, substitution and a high degree of rhythmical variation occur together coincide with the direct expression of adult detachment from the alluring beauty of the too-remote and artificial vision: "The vision still / Lies in the eye, soft blue and far away" and "That is illusion. The artificer / Of quiet, distance holds me in a vise . . . "

The more inclusive, "fallen" perspective is the effect, of course, of the experience presented in the second stanza. While from a distance the ocean is a static and tranquil *object* bounding the land, and a passive backdrop to the steamers that ply it, "firm in direction," up close it becomes a vital but uncontrollably destructive *energy*. Beyond the more violent diction, Winters rhythmically enacts this change by radically opening the initial couplet, and though the subsequent couplets remain relatively closed, the sentences are drawn so variously through them that the caesural pause is continually shifting to different positions within the lines. This, together with a more liberal use of substitution, enhances the sensation of an overwhelming power unamenable to human will.

The function which the meter performs here in the second stanza differs from the function it performs in the first. In the first stanza Winters associates the tidy, unruffled metrical norm with the false and overly artificial view of nature, a view whose coherence and harmony depend on distance remaking the external world into an image of desire. The rhythmical modifications of the metrical frame or "vise" represent the speaker's present-day and hard-earned detachment from that lulling dream. The rhythmical disruptions in the second stanza represent the invasion of mind by nature, the effect of which is to reduce the self to a more undifferentiated state; mind becomes mere "skull," consciousness (that which differentiates the human from the nonhuman) mere "dreaming hair." The metrical norm, by contrast, is the prosodic equivalent of the mind's need for order and stability. But if that order, that stabilitiy, is sustained in the first stanza by too great a distance from its irrational ground, here order is menaced by too much immersion in the irrational. The first two stanzas, in other words, present equally deficient extremes: on the one hand, the mind's projection of a static order that loses in vitality what it gains in illusory control, and on the other, a submission to flux, or irrational energy, that gives up in control and clarity what it gains in excitement or intensity.

The middle ground between these extremes is offered in the third stanza in the image of the "limber margin." This is Winters' moral as well as metrical ideal: an inclusive flexible position that participates in change without being given entirely over to it; a position where land and water, form and energy, thought and feeling, judgment and intense perception, the stability that comes of repetition, and the excitement that comes of surprise and variation, infuse without destroying one another. Winters explicitly asserts this position in the third stanza; but throughout the poem he implicitly enacts it in and through the metrical control. Even when the rhythm mimics or suggests the violent intermingling of self and sea, the metrical norm is still audible, never completely overcome or muted (the sense of violence being an illusory product of the metrical norm as the norm diminishes, without at the same time ever ceasing to be heard).

If we regard metrical control as the limber margin or outer boundary of awareness, then we can say that the meter represents the self's refusal to relinquish what enables it to measure, discriminate, and judge that chaotic wash of energy; the meter is the aural manifestation of the self's refusal to relinquish what keeps it separate from that sub-rational power. Meter, in other words, is the prosodic symbol of the distance consciousness requires to maintain itself in the presence of what it seeks to know. But the distance entails a trade-off: one gives up wholeness of being, complete absorption in experiential flux, and sheer intensity of sense perception for an always partial knowledge. This accounts in the last two stanzas for the complicated tone of affirmation of identity ("A landsman, I") and residual nostalgia for undifferentiated being ("The sea is but a sound. / I would be near it . . . "). Which is to say that in the closing lines (and indeed throughout the last two stanzas) there is just as much longing and fascination in the perception of the ocean as acknowledgment of danger and acceptance of limits. The sea is no longer a static object, forever standing "far out of sight," but rather a dynamic process that's as beautiful ("Heaving and wrinkled in the moon") as it is incomprehensible ("and blind, / Or gathers seaward, ebbing out of mind"). The "limber margin," prosodically as well as perceptually, may provide a vantage point from which the self can gain some knowledge of the unknown sources of its being, can bring the known and unknown into some sort of relation. But that knowledge, that relation, again, requires distance. And if one effect of distance is greater understanding, another is continued yearning for that which is forever ebbing out of mind.

There is no such residual romantic yearning in "The Cod Head."

Williams' seascape is a thoroughly disordered and disordering miscellany of debris and alien life. While "cod head" reminds us of godhead, and the red cross markings on the jellyfish evoke images of sacrifice and resurrection, they do so only to dramatize the unredeemable chaos of these northern waters. Williams establishes a more intimate relation than Winters to the external scene, closing the distance between observer and observed not in order to dissolve mind into nature, but rather to allow a keener, more refined attention to the distinction between the two. This greater intimacy, in turn, generates a cooler, less emotive, and more impersonal tone from which all traces of nostalgia have been utterly destroyed. What enables him to do this, I would argue, is the free verse line whose looser measure accommodates more generously the corrosive energies of nature. That is, the free verse enables us to feel both the externalizing formal pressure of imagination and the inflowing, chaotic wash. The shaping power of intelligence isn't suspended or abandoned so much as it's continually threatened and renewed by keeping as close as possible to what resists it. It's as if we witness, at every point within the poem, the first moment of creation when form emerges out of formlessness, when order resonates with the disorder it is drawn from. Prosodically, these dual pressures are enacted and sustained primarily in the lineation, in the counterpoint of sentence and line, sentence and stanza, with the linear and stanzaic markers representing the ordering nets of consciousness, and the syntax washing over those markers suggesting the unrestrainable violence of the waters. The non-numerically determined line enhances the mimetic power of the verse by enabling Williams to shift speed more dramatically than an iambic cadence would allow, quickening the rhythm by playing off clause, and even an individual word, against the line when he wants to show the violence and agitation of the water ("at night wildly / agitate phospores- / cent midges—"), and slowing the rhythm down with less radical enjambments when he wants to show the water's lulling calm ("—but by day / flaccid / moons in whose / discs sometimes a red cross / lives—").

But perhaps the association of the movement of the syntax with external scene, and the line and stanza with observing mind is much too neat. For the syntax itself expresses both, is suffused with both: through its restlessly enjambed and ever dissolving clauses that never achieve the closure or coherence they continually promise, the syntax becomes infected, as it were, with the uncontainable violence of the sea while at the same time conveying a keen awareness of the sea's alien nature, its menacing strangeness, its indifference to the human need to order and control. On the other hand, if the syntax is suggestive of the sea in the way it holds in random association all the miscellaneous details and contrary motions which the speaker's eye takes in—the violence of whipping oars, the calm of the jelly fish ("flaccid moons"), the falling and lifting cod heads, etc.—it also enacts the form-seeking energies of the observer, tracing in its sequence of clauses the subtle arc of his attention from surface to depth, then back to surface, imposing or attempting to impose a human measure on that alien world ("four / fathom . . . three fathom / . . . and now . . . "). And even here, in the calling out of the fathoms, one feels both the human rage for order in the brief sequence of numbers, and the unorderable confusion of the sea itself in the floating positions those numbers occupy within and between the lines.

Winters' commitment to meter proceeds from the belief that the more porous the boundary between the mind and world, the greater the risk of disintegration. If the refuge form provides becomes too static, though, too removed from the flow of circumstance, one runs the opposite risk of imperception, the dead, mechanical monotony of habit or routine ("The land is numb . . ."). A metrical norm measures and controls the variations worked around it, and thereby provides the limber margin from which the known, the old, the expected, is put in contact with but never obliterated by the new, the unknown, the unforeseen. Williams subscribes to the same view but he extends the limber margin farther out into that alien element. He expresses an almost aboriginal faith in the mind's ability to navigate uncharted waters, to open itself up to the unknown and still compel the unknown into meaningful shape. The more improvisatory rhythms of free verse allow him to keep pace with the flux of nature and also, as he does so, to assert the human need for organizing structure, so that at every moment in the poem mind is trembling with chaos, and chaos with mind, not in order to dissolve the boundary between the two but rather to explore with greater specificity the differences between them.

6. Let's say that the poet writing in meter, working out of an already-established set of conventions, is tacitly committed to a social or historical countenance even when he turns to immediate experience,

while the poet writing in free verse, dispensing with those conventions, is tacitly committed to an individual or immediate countenance even when he turns to history, to social life.

7. The poet writing in meter is always the belated one, the bearer of other lives, Aeneas with Anchises on his back, the one whose origins and ends are always elsewhere. His is the speech of the finite self, already fallen from Edenic plenitude into language and time, recollection and anticipation, bounded by what D. H. Lawrence calls the infinite past and the infinite future. And his metrical symmetries, arising from "the full, yearning flow of aspiration" and "the sweet, poignant ebb of remembrance and regret," are the persistent echoes of the gate of Eden closing shut behind him.

8. The poet writing in free verse, on the other hand, claims for himself the Adamic privilege of starting over, of seeing the world again as on the morning of the first day. In Lawrence's terms, his is a poetry of the sheer present, the incarnate now, neither fixed star nor pearl but living plasma, the quick of life itself whose open measures correspond to "the rapid momentaneous association of things which meet and pass on the forever incalculable journey of creation. . . . "

9. Though the poet writing in meter expresses a communal allegiance in deciding to write in an already-established form, he doesn't follow that allegiance passively or complacently; rather he tests it at every point (in the interplay of norm and variation, metrical pattern and fluidities of speech, syntax and line, or syntax and stanza) so as to discover how much individual expression, how much freedom, how much novelty of perception, he can accommodate and still remain within a world intelligible to others. The social countenance implicit in traditional meter, in other words, reveals or is made to reveal the disfiguring, presocial, never entirely domesticated energies behind it, energies that resist, require, and renew the very form, the very countenance, that is expressing them.

10. Likewise, the aim of free verse is not unmediated experience, a merely passive rendering of flux. The writer of free verse doesn't distrust any and all forms of mediation in the interest of presenting life in all its pristine freshness; rather he minimizes the mediating elements in order to make each moment of composition a reiteration of the creation itself, of light being called forth out of darkness, order out of flux. The belief implicit in every free verse poem is that the mind can return to the originating moment of its own emergence, so as to reenact the process of its fall.

11. The belief implicit in every metrical poem is that the mind is unredeemably historical, and can only look back, as it were, with longing and relief, at what it had to give up to get where it is.

1991

Part 3

"Far Lamps at Night": The Poetry of J. V. Cunningham

In 1974, my senior year at Brandeis University, I studied poetry writing with Galway Kinnell and J. V. Cunningham. Kinnell was that year's poet in residence and taught the undergraduate writing class, which I took spring semester. Cunningham was of course a permanent member of the Brandeis English department and, though he was on leave that spring, I would bring him poems now and then and he would criticize them. Studying poetry with Kinnell and Cunningham was like studying political science with Jerry Rubin (pre–Wall Street) and William F. Buckley. The political analogy is apt for we had not yet pulled our troops from Vietnam, and in the highly charged political climate of the student-led antiwar movement, even literary questions and choices became or were considered political in a very narrow sense. Kinnell, for instance, refused to let his students write anything but free verse on the grounds that rhyme and meter repress emotion and free verse liberates it. Oddly enough, his defense of free verse and liberated feeling was deterministic, based on a kind of evolutionary theory:

> I guess that Elizabethans, for instance, sensed some lovely repetitiveness about existence. The rhymes in their poems are a way of acknowledging the everlasting return of things. A harmony sounded through time. The formal aspects of their poems were ways of sharing in it, perhaps of propitiating it. Most of us moderns hear nothing like that. When we listen we hear outer space telling us we're a race living for a while on a little planet that will die.[1]

The assumption implicit here is that the significance of literary forms is necessarily tied to the historical circumstances in which those forms arise. When circumstances change, forms either adapt by changing into something else or ossify. The argument that literary forms are culturally conditioned has a long history. We can think, for instance, of Milton rebelling against "the bondage of rhyme," which he regard-

ed as "the invention of a barbarous age," or of Wordsworth's rejec-
tion of neoclassic decorum, of an overly specialized poetic language
tied to the upper class and disassociated from the speech habits and
experiences of the common man. Yet neither Milton nor Wordsworth
saw the literary past as a junkyard of obsolete modes of expression
but rather as an expressive resource from which they could select
some forms and reject others according to their needs and interests.
In attacking the artificiality of certain formal conventions, they were
in no way attacking formality itself or metrical regularity.

Nor would Milton nor Wordsworth have made a simple corre-
spondence between the form one writes in and the way one votes. To
Kinnell, however, free verse is the literary equivalent of progressive
democratic thinking, and traditional form becomes associated with
political conservatism—"with those who feel one shouldn't poke
under the surface, that one shouldn't tempt the gods or invite trouble,
that one should be content to live with his taboos unchallenged, with
his repressions and politeness unquestioned; that just as the highest
virtues in the state are law and order, so the highest virtue in poetry
is formality and morality."[2] Hence, to choose free verse over formal
verse is to choose curiosity over conformity, natural feeling over cold-
blooded rationality, perception-transcending custom over quietist
acceptance of the status quo. It was on these assumptions that Kinnell
objected to a rhymed poem I turned in to class one day because, as he
put it, "Rhyme denies truth." Later when I met with Cunningham, I
told him what Kinnell had said, and with wry amusement, as though
this were not the first time he had heard this, he replied, "Well, I
don't doubt it. But there are some truths worth denying."

To anyone familiar with his work, this is a typical Cunningham
remark, for he is in an important sense a poet of denials—a metrical
formalist in a time when free verse has become the norm; a philo-
sophical poet trafficking in ideas and propositions at a time when a
poem should not mean but be. He does not believe, as Denise Lever-
tov does, that "the poet does not *use* poetry, but is at the service of
poetry"; nor does he subscribe to the concept of the poet as bardic
savage, the Kinnellian primitive for whom poetry is "that sticky infu-
sion, that rank flavor of blood." Rather poetry for Cunningham is a
social activity whose methods and standards are those of craftsman-
ship and whose concerns are for the ordinary human self.[3] In keeping
with these concerns, Cunningham's principal but by no means exclu-
sive style is the plain style, the models of which are the familiar letter

or urbane conversation; it is a style whose effects Cunningham has characterized as "noticeably unnoticeable, a quietness so apt it is heard."[4] Unmannered and consequently restricted neither to the mysterious images of surrealism nor to sensory detail—but capable of accommodating both—the style can affirm as well as present, argue as well as imagine. Perhaps the only restriction on the style's flexibility is that it should never seem more noticeable than the content. In this sense, it is the stylistic equivalent of rapt attentiveness or unselfconscious concentration on the object of concern, even if the object is the self. To adapt a Buddhist saying, when the plain stylist is pointing to the moon, he wants us to see the moon, not the pointing finger.[5]

Yet the plain style should not be confused with what Mark Strand calls the international style, a bland, homogenized transcendence of personality. Cunningham's poems are unmistakably his own. The intelligence that animates his work is fiercely individual, intending at almost every turn to upset our expectations that the idea of a poem should be commonplace or unimportant, its expression original. He is constantly reminding us that his poems are his, not ours, "that these were his circumstances, not yours; and these were the structures of thought by which he had penetrated them."[6] The style becomes the medium through which he can make known to us these structures of thought and feeling; it can express even eccentricities of individual thinking without being itself eccentric.

From the literary evolutionary point of view, the plain style and metrical formality are at best innocuous anachronisms. Each new generation of writers has to forge from actual experience new forms and new styles so that their poems can reflect as well as articulate the changing historical moment. Free verse is now the norm because it's thought to be more adaptable to individual expression, more improvisatory. Yet this pursuit of the moment in style as well as content has fostered its own kind of uniformity; it has resulted in a standardized casualness of form and diction and, perhaps to overcompensate for this apparent familiarity or languor, a search for the striking image or metaphor, such that altered expression is an end in itself, mannerism the mark of authenticity.

> I would love to give myself back to the night
> so that my naked body could become inarticulate
> but loud like the sun.
> I'm tired of thinking about myself . . .[7]

With crayons and pieces of paper, I entered the empty room.
I sat on the floor and drew pictures all day.
One day I held a picture against the bare wall:
It was a window. Climbing through,

I stood in a sloping field
at dusk. As I began walking, night settled.
Far ahead in the valley, I saw the lights
of a village, and always, at my back, I felt
the white room swallowing what was passed.[8]

In the first example, one may wonder in what sense the sun is loud.
This unimaginable figure, which the poet claims to be able to imagine
by mere assertion of poetic authenticity, serves only to remind us that
this is, after all, a poem, despite the bland, proselike rhythms of the
lines. What qualifies the monotonously simple sentences in the second
example is the somewhat spooky metamorphosis of the drawing into a
window, through which the poet climbs, and the ominous metaphor in
the last line. In both cases the line is nothing but a linear and gram-
matical backdrop across which now and then strange images and
details wander in loose association. What originality the two poems
possess resides entirely within the idiosyncrasies of style. And yet
their idiosyncrasies are similar—part of a standard fare, a new con-
vention, and so hardly idiosyncrasies at all.

Cunningham's style, on the other hand, is seldom striking; his
originality lies in the effect of what he has to say, what his style makes
plain. It is a style capable of defining the particulars of time and place
without being confined to them. His poems articulate and dramatize
a twentieth-century sensibility, with twentieth-century concerns. But
he differs from the two poets just quoted, and from his own contem-
poraries such as e.e. cummings and Dylan Thomas, in being only a
child, not a disciple, of his times.

A good introduction to his work is epigram 19:

When I shall be without regret
And shall mortality forget,
When I shall die who lived for this,
I shall not miss the things I miss.
And you who notice where I lie
Ask not my name. It is not I.[9]

The language is abstract, unambiguous, free of imagery and figures of speech. The poem's suggestiveness comes from our familiarity with the conventions of the epitaph and the expectations which that familiarity creates. From past experience we expect that all epitaphs will state the name of the deceased and give one or two summary details about the past life, as in this funny epitaph on a dentist: "Reader, approach this grave with gravity: / John Brown has filled his last cavity." But notice how Cunningham upsets these expectations by withholding the name and saying nothing about the life. The point of the poem lies in our disappointed expectations, for by means of them he not only conveys his individual perception that death is the total obliteration of personality (rendering everything about the past life irrelevant) but also manages to set that perception off against the traditional ideas about death implicit in the epitaph conventions.

I am using the term "convention" here to stand for any principle governing the selection and arrangement of material within a poem, and this includes thematic as well as technical elements. A poem is going to embody several kinds of conventions or norms of expectation—if it's a letter poem, we automatically expect it to be one half of a dialogue; if it's a love poem, that it will have something to do with a relationship; if it's iambically cadenced, we expect light and heavy syllables to alternate, just as if it's free verse, we expect them to avoid this alternation. I don't mean to suggest that poems are generated merely by conventions rather than by some lived experience. "No one will deny," Cunningham has remarked,

> what is overwhelmingly obvious, the immediacy and absoluteness in itself of one's primary experience. But this is by definition self-sealed, isolated, and incommunicable . . . . To speak or to think or to write is to go beyond this . . . . For to write is to confront one's primary experience with the externally objective: first, with the facts of experience and with the norms of possibility and probability of experience; secondly, with the objective commonality of language and literary forms. To be successful in this enterprise is to integrate the subjectively primary, the immediate, with the objectively communicable, the mediate, to the alteration of both by their conformation to each other, by their connexity with and their immanence in

> each other. It is the conquest of solipsism, the dra-
> matic conflict of self with, on the one hand, reality in
> all its objectivity and potentiality, and, on the other,
> with philology in its old and general sense: or, with
> private and with public history.[10]

To use Cunningham's terms, convention is the mediate, whereas
the immediate or the subjectively primary is that which resists, qual-
ifies, or individualizes that structure of mediation, to the alteration of
both. So in Ben Jonson's epigram, "On My First Son," the resigna-
tion Jonson feels or ought to feel as a Christian is qualified by the grief
he does feel as a father. If the conventions of Christian resignation
prevent his grief from becoming excessive, the immediacy of grief pre-
vents the resignation from being too pat, too conventional. And this
tension is reflected in the metrical conventions where the heavily
stressed syllables—coordinate with the speaker's grief—upset (with-
out overthrowing) the iambic norm ("O, could I loose all father now,
for why").[11]

No convention, obviously, can contain the whole of an experience.
Truth will always have its jagged edges. But the more sharply defined
a convention is, the more sharply perceptible those jagged edges can
appear, modifying or resisting the conventions necessary for their
articulation. It is these modifications and resistances that interest
Cunningham, that form the vital heart of his best work. In poems and
epigrams alike, his method is to distinguish the limits of convention by
defining the ways in which his own experience alters it, and is altered
by it. And this can take any number of forms. He can, for instance,
make some unconventional turn on a conventional idea, so as to real-
ize the truth of it in a way that changes its original meaning, as in epi-
gram 15 where the old saw, "time heals all wounds," as he defines it no
longer offers consolation:

> Deep summer, and time pauses. Sorrow wastes
> To a new sorrow. While time heals time hastes.

In epigram 51, he works the same disquieting change upon the com-
monplace, "all things come to those who wait":

> All in due time: love will emerge from hate,

And the due deference of truth from lies.
If not quite all things come to those who wait
They will not need them: in due time one dies.

Or he can define himself against some assumed value or received
idea. Where you and I might thrive on the expectation of disaster as
a source of bliss and as a proof of our virility, Cunningham prefers
indifference:

If wisdom, as it seems it is,
Be the recovery of some bliss
From the conditions of disaster—
Terror the servant, man the master—
It does not follow we should seek
Crises to prove ourselves unweak.
Much of our lives, God knows, is error,
But who will trifle with unrest?
These fools who would solicit terror,
Obsessed with being unobsessed,
Professionals of experience
Who have disasters to withstand them
As if fear never had unmanned them,
Flaunt a presumptuous innocence.

I have preferred indifference.[12]

Unless we can step outside our assumptions that a poem should not be
argumentative or logical, or that a poet should not mean what he says,
we will miss the subtle interplay of form and content—the way, for
instance, Cunningham uses the line to emphasize the logic of his argu-
ment; or the way the long penultimate sentence sets up by contrast the
closing line's declaration which, grammatically self-contained, sug-
gests the emotional detachment it asserts; or the way the clever rhyme
of innocence and experience almost announces that the argument has
made these antonyms synonymous.

Perhaps our greatest difficulty with the poem, however, comes
from our surprise at finding intellectual wit and anger so compatible.
In so much of our poetry of outrage (however well-intentioned), poets

have felt compelled to sacrifice intelligence, that power to compare and weigh the value of competing ideas or images, for emotional intensity, as though intelligence were the mark of insincerity, or anger a kind of antinomian transcendence of ordinary moral categories. But here there is no such exclusivity. Though Cunningham concentrates into a single definition a type of character that could take any number of forms (skiers, mountain climbers, do-gooders, even certain confessional poets), what keeps the poem from being mere superficial labeling is the reference to his own encounters with unmanning fear and disaster, implicit in his definition of fools who would solicit terror. Because he knows from experience that life is disastrous enough, that "sorrow wastes / to a new sorrow," he prefers indifference to trifling with unrest. (Or, as he says in "Autumn," another poem about indifference, *But say what moralist / Shall in himself subsist? / The tried.*") In other words, the speaker's intelligence— dramatized within the subtleties of form—sustains and legitimizes his indignation by implicating the personal experience behind it. The definition is not a precept or rubric; it is not merely a momentary clarification abstracted and insulated from experience. Rather it continually points us back to the experiences it's drawn from, experiences where no such insularity exists, except perhaps for the presumptuously innocent, and then not even for them: "Much of our lives, God knows, is error."

Another method of Cunningham's is to bring the properties of one convention to bear on an experience not normally associated with that convention, so as both to illuminate the experience by defining what it isn't and to revitalize the convention by using it in some new way, as seen in "Montana Pastoral":

> I am no shepherd of a child's surmises.
> I have seen fear where the coiled serpent rises.
>
> Thirst where the grasses burn in early May
> And thistle, mustard, and the wild oat stay.
>
> There is dust in this air. I saw in the heat
> Grasshoppers busy in the threshing wheat.
>
> So to this hour. Through the warm dusk I drove
> To blizzards sifting on the hissing stove,

> And found no images of pastoral will,
> But fear, thirst, hunger, and this huddled chill.

Cunningham establishes here a double frame of reference whereby he both describes the harsh Montana landscape of his youth and, at the same time, keeps one eye on the idealized world of English pastoral verse. Like Marvell's "The Garden" or Jonson's "To Penshurst," his pastoral is in couplets. But whereas theirs present a prelapsarian unity with nature in which all things come effortlessly to man for his enjoyment, his presents a landscape of deprivation, estrangement, and labor; if all is sweetness and light in Marvell and Jonson's world, there is dust in the air in this one; if that landscape answers to a child's surmise, this one remains stubbornly literal, despite whatever pastoral will one brings to it. And so he can feel only what the more conventional pastoral world excludes: fear, thirst, hunger, and this huddled chill.

In a sense, this landscape represents a vision of experience (underlying many of his poems) as penury, as loss and disappointment—a vision in which the ideal of fulfillment is a child's surmise. And yet it is a state he values. For if the fear, thirst, and hunger of experience require stoical detachment, if they make separateness necessary for survival, that separateness in turn can nourish consciousness; that standing apart from others, even from his own experience, can sharpen awareness to a bladelike clarity which in the midst of loss and betrayal can preserve the self. So in the epigram "Towards Tucson" he can write, "In this attractive desolation, / A world's debris framed by a fence, / Drink is my only medication / And loneliness is my defense."

In this respect Cunningham has strong affinities with Emily Dickinson. Like her, he values above all else that almost querulously individual capacity to know and understand ("This consciousness that is aware"), preferring clear thinking over the comforts of received wisdom or warm illusions, even if what one thinks clearly about is how ultimately illusory one's thinking is.[13] And since the price for this insistence on awareness is isolation—in that to be aware of something is to stand outside it—isolation (Dickinson's "Columnar self") becomes a kind of guardian angel (789). Compare, for instance, Dickinson's "It might be lonelier without the loneliness" with Cunningham's "Timor Dei." In both poems the speaker regards the absolute as an annihilating force. Though Dickinson's rejection of it is less

definitive (because more speculative) than Cunningham's, she
nonetheless implies that oneness with God would amount to a dese-
cration of her loneliness, a violation of the self-definition loneliness
bestows:

> It might be lonelier
> Without the Loneliness—
> I'm so accustomed to my Fate
> Perhaps the Other—Peace—
>
> Would interrupt the Dark—
> And crowd the little Room—
> Too scant—by Cubits—to contain
> The Sacrament of Him—
>
> I am not used to Hope—
> It might intrude upon—
> Its sweet parade—blaspheme the place—
> Ordained for Suffering—
>
> It might be easier
> to fail—with Land in Sight—
> Than gain—my Blue Peninsula—
> And perish—of Delight.

So she prefers a state of knowing deprivation, of suffering awareness
("to fail—with Land in Sight"), to an annihilating peace or fulfillment
that would cancel the need for knowing ("And perish—of Delight").

So too in "Timor Dei" the absolute is lethal, "as pervasive, as
destructively absorbent as sensation, or passion, or sympathy."[14]
"Timor Dei" also represents another example of Cunningham's skill
in putting conventional materials to unconventional ends. For though
it is a rejection of God, it is cast in the form of a prayer:

> Most beautiful, most dear,
> When I would use Thy light,
> Beloved, omniscient Seer,
> Thou didst abuse my sight.
>
> Thou didst pervade my being

Like marsh air steeped in brine;
Thou didst invade my seeing
Till all I saw was Thine.

Today, from my own fence
I saw the grass fires rise,
And saw Thine old incense
Borne up in frosty sighs.

Most terrible, most rude,
I will not shed a tear
For lost beatitude,
But I still fear Thy fear.

The poem turns on the theme of seeing; to see something requires the capacity to discriminate, and discrimination requires distance. But the absolute, by definition, cannot be discriminated or comprehended or seen, and thus is terrifying to a poet so passionate about clarity of thought and perception. Only when the speaker is fenced off, protected from the absolute by his separateness, or self-consciousness, can he see the grass fires rise, and see in the sense of understanding or intellectual perception (signaled by the repetition of "saw") "Thine old incense / Borne up in frosty sighs." What I find so remarkable about this image is the way it brings together the beautiful and terrible aspects of the absolute, for if "Thine old incense / Borne up" suggests the attractiveness of acquiescence, "frosty sighs" suggests the mortal dangers of it, the self-consuming nature of this awe.

This is no simple rejection, in other words, because the old patterns of thought and feeling still persist (though his belief is gone) and still have power to overwhelm him. The last stanza provides the most moving example of this ambivalence. Though it consists of a single sentence, that sentence reverses its direction in the last line, turning from the almost prideful claim that he will not shed a tear for lost beatitude to the concluding acknowledgment, "But I still fear Thy fear." That the last line grammatically qualifies the previous assertion might encourage us to read it only as a kind of grudging concession that the speaker is not entirely free or protected. And yet because it sounds the last note in the poem, it seems conclusive, implying that the power of this fearful awe is not amenable to reason or rational control, however much he wants it to be.

The same ambivalence lies behind "The Phoenix," an unusual poem for Cunningham in that he implies, rather than states, his theme through a succession of symbolic details:

> More than the ash stays you from nothingness!
> Nor here nor there is a consuming pyre!
> Your essence is in infinite regress
> That burns with varying consistent fire,
> Mythical bird that bears in burying!
>
> I have not found you in exhausted breath
> That carves its image on the Northern air,
> I have not found you on the glass of death
> Though I am told that I shall find you there,
> Imperturbable in the final cold,
>
> There where the North wind shapes white cenotaphs,
> There where snowdrifts cover the fathers' mound,
> Unmarked but for these wintry epitaphs,
> Still are you singing there without sound,
> Your mute voice on the crystal embers flinging.

Cunningham argues here against the doctrine of regeneration in terms that dramatize his emotional attachment to it, clinging to an idea his experiences have, if anything, refuted. The effect of this tension is that the phoenix seems present and absent at the same time, his denial an affirmation of a sort, as the long concluding sentence shifts from the disappointed expectations ("I have not found you") to the assertion of the presence of the phoenix in the closing lines: the mythical bird is there, so his religious tradition tells him and so he would like to believe, but it is imperceptible to human sense, singing without sound. This elusiveness of being present to desire but absent to sense is even reflected in the internal rhymes that end each stanza: as John Baxter observes, being partially hidden the rhymes suggest the bird's elusive presence—there but imperceptible; yet they also dramatize its absence in that we can hear the rhymes but cannot hear the "mute voice on the crystal embers flinging."[15]

Cunningham's restless need for self-defining separateness is also implicated, as it is for Dickinson, in his need for love and his capacity for loving others. His love poems fall between two extremes. At one end is love as that respect for another person independent of desires and needs, that selfless attention whereby we recognize the other on the other's terms. It is a state, needless to say, one has to struggle to achieve, and even then achieves only for privileged moments, as when Cunningham says in what I think is the climactic moment in "To What Strangers What Welcome": "It's that I care more for you / Than for my feeling for you." At the other extreme is love as the narcissistic feeling of being in love, that state of passion or desire in which the object is incidental to the fulfillment. This state resembles the vague, indefinable potential of the absolute; Cunningham describes it in "The Journal of John Cardan" as "an emanation of the indeterminable sources of personal identity, a void region of possibilities where dwells the promise of multiple and unrestricted fulfillments."[16] So also in "Passion" he calls it "pure unact / . . . all the loves that swarm / In the unwilled to be." In this state, we want to possess or modify the object of desire, to reduce it to a mirror of the self. To love at that other extreme, however, is to desire without wanting to modify; it is to consent to distance, as Simone Weil remarks, to adore the distance between ourselves and that which we love, and so implies a renunciation.[17] Cunningham provides a marvelous example of such a renunciation in his essay on "Ideal Fiction":

> So in Sidney's episode of Argalus, and Parthenia, the hopeless and constant lover, offered an exact replica of his love—indeed it is Parthenia herself, unidentified—courteously declines. "It is only happiness I refuse, since of the only happiness I could and can desire I am refused." He is in love with her identity.[18]

This is, of course, an extreme case. But even an imperfect regard for another person means to live divided against oneself, for "only the selfishly insane can integrate experience to the heart's desires, and only the emotionally sterile would not wish to."[19] To love in this way, neither giving in to one's wayward wishes nor denying them, is to value distance and desire, judgment and immediacy, though the balance between the two, as seen in "The Beacon," is never perfect:

> Men give their hearts away;
> Whether for good or ill
> They cannot say

Who shape the object in their will.

The will in pure delight
conceives itself. I praise
     Far lamps at night,
Cold landmarks for reflection's gaze.

Distant they remain,
Oh, unassailed, apart!
     May time attain
The promise ere death seals the heart!

Cunningham defines a serious human problem akin to T. S. Eliot's
concept of the dissociation of sensibility, though the traditional lan-
guage here and the unlocalized context indicate that Cunningham
does not think of it as a problem peculiar to the modern world.
Though he praises "Far lamps at night, / Cold landmarks for reflec-
tion's gaze," preferring (like Dickinson) self-denial in the interest of
awareness over self-delight, he recognizes the serious incompleteness
of this way of loving. So with desperate urgency ("Oh, unassailed,
apart!"), he prays for an integration of emotion and reflection. He
wants to possess the loved one in an immediate way without sacrific-
ing the powers of judgment; which is to say, he wants to be able to
appropriate as well as to distinguish. But, again, this is presented
only as a hope for the future. That he would praise in the meantime,
in his dissociated state, discrimination over sensation, the far lamps
over his own delight, is a measure of Cunningham's generosity, of his
desire to care more for the object of his concern than for his feeling
for it.[20]
     Even when the object of his concern is his own feelings, he exer-
cises the same generous care, such that the poem never merely imi-
tates an emotion; it never seems, for example, as desperate in style as
it is in theme. The intelligence that controls the expression is larger
than the particular state of mind it expresses (another manifestation
of his need for self-defining separateness, even from aspects of the
self); this doesn't mean the feeling is weak or automatically must with-
er in the cold blast of intellect. "The judge is fury," Cunningham has
written. Without intensity of feeling or concern no poem could com-
pel our interest. But what it does mean is that the style in his best
poems, animated by a passionate intelligence, can comprehend the

most passionate emotions with no loss of intensity, and can thereby make those emotions comprehensible to us. So "The Aged Lover Discourses in the Flat Style" manages to articulate a state of sexual isolation without being isolated itself or sealed off from our understanding:

> There are, perhaps, whom passion gives a grace,
> Who fuse and part as dancers on the stage,
> But that is not for me, not at my age,
> Not with my bony shoulders and fat face.
> Yet in my clumsiness I found a place
> And use for passion: with it I ignore
> My gaucheries and yours, and feel no more
> The awkwardness of the absurd embrace.
>
> It is a pact men make, and seal in flesh,
> To be so busy with their own desires
> Their loves may be as busy with their own,
> And not in union. Though the two enmesh
> Like gears in motion, each with each conspires
> To be at once together and alone.

Like "Montana Pastoral," "The Aged Lover" uses an old convention in a new way. A perfect Petrarchan sonnet, it associates itself with the sixteenth-century Petrarchan sonnets that celebrated idealized love in what C. S. Lewis calls the sweet style. But all Cunningham retains of that tradition is the form, for the style is flat, not sweet, in the urbane manner of Shakespeare's sonnet 138 ("When my love swears that she is made of truth") or in Jonson's "My Picture Left in Scotland." Thus Cunningham asserts the individual experience of love by combining the flat style with a form associated with the sweet.

To appreciate the poem fully we ought to look briefly at Jonson's "My Picture Left in Scotland," as Cunningham quietly alludes to it in a way that fuses the conventional with the personal, and a reader, unfamiliar with Jonson's poem, might think Cunningham is being merely personal when in fact he's being both. In "My Picture Left in Scotland," Jonson, the aged (and hence unconventional) lover, wonders if love is rather deaf than blind (twisting a cliché, as Cunningham so often does) because the woman he adores so much has not been moved by his graceful language. But then he realizes that the cause of her indifference is:

> . . . that she hath seen
> My hundred of grey hairs,
> Told seven-and-forty years,
> Read so much waste, as she cannot embrace
> My mountain belly, and my rocky face;
> And all these through her eyes have stopped her ears.[21]

Cunningham's poem is even flatter, less adorned than Jonson's. But the few rhetorical touches—his bony shoulders and fat face echoing Jonson's mountain belly and rocky face, and the figure of the dancers for whom passion gives a grace versus the figure of the gears in motion for him and his lover—stand out all the more effectively against the plainer background. Likewise, the subtle way Cunningham plays the sentence against the line further qualifies the plainness. I have in mind especially the breaks between lines 5 and 6, and 11 and 12. In the first instance, by breaking the line between "place" and "use" he demonstrates the compartmentalization he describes, increasing the sense of passion as something he self-consciously manipulates toward an unself-conscious end ("with it I ignore / My gaucheries and yours"). In the second instance, line 11 forms a complete clause and could stand on its own; the additional phrase "And not in union" comes almost as a surprise, though it is in fact a logical consequence of what's just been said. By ending the sentence after "union" Cunningham further isolates the phrase, reinforcing the implicit definition of intimacy as a kind of shared estrangement.

One can find the same masterful use of form in "Monday Morning," a deceptively unassuming poem about emotional and psychological blandness which, like "The Aged Lover," is written in a flat style. In fact, the flatness here is even more extreme, for the poem is in syllabic meter, a more casual measure closer to the speaker's flatness of mood. Yet like "The Aged Lover," "Monday Morning" succeeds in dramatizing this flatness without being flat itself. One way it avoids this is through an unobtrusive yet remarkable compression of language and detail that implicates a coherent story in a few lines. As the speaker goes out to check his mail, a woman passes, and he tries (unsuccessfully) to construe the meeting as sexually resonant:

> The flattery has been infrequent
> And somewhat grudging. There is junk mail

And no letter. The weather cloudy
With more snow. Fortuitous meeting,
The rustle of flirtation, the look—
Self-esteem sustained by any excuse,
By any misconstruction? No. No.
It is now a January world,
An after Christmas waiting. For what?
Not for this snow, this silence. There is
No resonance in the universe.
I must buy something extra today
And clutter up my house and my life.

One striking thing about this encounter is that the woman is never directly mentioned but rather appears obliquely through the haze of his subjective misconstructions. Cunningham renders his subjective isolation with startling immediacy, yet at the same time he moves beyond it to the realization that his misconstructions are misconstructions, not fact. He dramatizes this process of realization with the line breaks, moving from the assertion of sexual possibility in one line ("The rustle of flirtation, the look") to the questions which deflate this possibility in the next ("Self-esteem sustained by any excuse, / By any misconstruction?"). Throughout the poem Cunningham sustains the same witty tension between the line and sentence whereby every enjambed phrase qualifies, by deflating, the meaning of the previous line, creating a kind of bad news / worse news effect. If the flattery has been infrequent, at least there has been flattery; but what small consolation this provides the next line takes away ("And somewhat grudging"); just as the last line, "And clutter up my house and my life," destroys whatever solace we thought the decision to buy something extra today might give. This psychological process—dramatized by the line breaks—of seeking consolation which his sullen clarity won't allow would be lost if the poem were written out as prose; that is, the form is crucially, even organically, part of the content. It is not a bottle into which he pours his perceptions and insights but the medium through which he discovers them.

It is our misfortune that Cunningham is not more highly esteemed than he is, or at least better known. Part of our difficulty with him is that we're conditioned by the specialized nature of our cultural and historical circumstances to think about literature in exclusive dichotomies: public versus private, objective versus subjective, thought versus feeling, propositions about experience versus experience itself, and so on. In keeping with this specializing habit, the aesthetic assumptions which underlie many of the literary movements of the past hundred years have been reductive in nature; whether we have in mind the symbolist poetics of Mallarmé, the postsymbolist poetics of Ashbery, Plath's confessionalism, or Strand's surrealism, much of the literary theory and practice of the modern and postmodern period has attempted to purify art of all traces of utilitarianism and rationality. This tendency has fostered experiments and innovations that have greatly enriched the possibilities of language. And for this we should be grateful. But the proscriptions that have accompanied these practices—no ideas but in things, a poem should not mean but be, rhyme denies truth—would banish from the page almost everything but the moment itself, the evanescent image.

If we glance casually at Cunningham's work, at the seemingly tightfisted little poems, all in meter, most in rhyme, many of them entirely abstract and philosophical, we might conclude that he subscribes to this dualistic thinking, seeking an intellectual refuge from the unmanageable indeterminacies of experience where many of his contemporaries seek an emotional and experiential refuge from the intellect. But poets such as Kinnell or Levertov reveal their modern prejudices in assuming that the presence of intellectual exactitude of statement means an absence of intensity of feeling, or that metrical formality is predictably mechanical and safe, and free verse necessarily open, spontaneous, and risky. As I have tried to show, Cunningham's method is inclusive, despite "the exclusions of a rhyme" or the hard-edged definitiveness. In his hands form becomes a supple instrument of exploration and expression, capable of implicating through the variations of rhyme and meter, and line and sentence, the subtle contours of emotion underlying thought or the resistant vagueness of experience that clarity must push against. His respect for form and convention is motivated by an almost finicky need to assert his individual way of looking at the world, to remind us that the poems are his, not ours. The relationship between convention and experience is not antagonistic but compatible: if his immediate experience individualizes the convention, the convention also socializes, as it were, or makes communicable, that immediacy. So the Petrarchan sonnet form of "The Aged Lover" organizes his unconventional isolation in the context of love into the conventional octave and sestet; yet that isolation particularizes this sonnet structure, making it unlike any other sonnet ever written. The poem is traditional and original, familiar and new.

But the prevailing conventions of our day are exclusive, not inclusive, developing certain necessary ingredients of the literary act to the exclusion of other equally necessary ingredients. As ingredients, spontaneity and uniqueness are essential, but as exclusive driving forces they have hardened into a narrow orthodoxy of fleeting whispers and unexamined cries—naked bodies loud like the sun and that rank flavor of blood. The poetry that dominates the literary periodicals can improvise the moment, but it does little else. And the moment, "the mere interrogation of immediate consciousness," Alfred North Whitehead has observed, "tells us very little. Analytic thinking vanishes under such direct scrutiny. We have recourse to memory, to the testimony of others, including their memories, to language in the form of the analysis of words and phrases—which is to say, to etymology and syntax. We should also consider the institutions of mankind in the light of an embodiment of their stable experiences."[22] The plain style and metrical formality—the literary equivalents of stability and continuity—have liberated Cunningham (without cutting him off) from the tyranny of the moment and the mannerisms such a tyranny imposes. For if change is a constant in our experience, so is continuity and repetition. What makes Cunningham so central and valuable is his capacity to accommodate both without restricting himself to either.

We like to think we value originality; but originality has had to take a predictable form for us to see it. Ironically, the assumption that all poets should be new and different has cheated us of seeing a poet who conforms to none of our expectations, who is genuinely new and different, and who deserves the same kind of concentrated, generous attention which his own work exemplifies.

1983

Notes

1. Galway Kinnell, *Walking Down the Stairs* (Ann Arbor, Mich., 1978), 29.

2. Kinnell, "Poetry, Personality, and Death," *Field* 4 (Spring 1971): 67. For a fine discussion of this sort of specious politicizing of poetic form, see Paul Breslin, "What the Signs of Promise Are," *Ploughshares* 7, no. 2 (1981): 150–65.

3. Denise Levertov, "The Poet in the World," in *The Poet in the World* (New York, 1973), 115; Kinnell, "The Bear," in *Body Rags* (London, 1969), 63; see J. V. Cunningham, "The Quest of the Opal," in *The Collected Essays of J. V. Cunningham* (Athens, Oh., 1977), 407.

4. Cunningham, "The Styles and Procedures of Wallace Stevens," in *Collected Essays*, 395.

5. I owe this Buddhist saying to Kenneth Fields, who uses it in a work in progress on Yvor Winters.

6. Cunningham, "Quest of the Opal," in *Collected Essays*, 407.

7. Marcia Southwick, from "Soon This Poem Will Become Transparent," in *The Night Won't Save Anyone* (Athens, Ga., 1980), 55.

8. Gregory Orr, "The Room," in *Burning the Empty Nets* (New York, 1973), 15.

9. Cunningham, *Collected Poems and Epigrams of J. V. Cunningham* (Athens, Oh., 1971), 112. All further poems and epigrams of Cunningham that are quoted may be found in this work.

10. Cunningham, "The Journal of John Cardan," in *Collected Essays*, 427.

11. Ben Jonson, "On My First Son," in *Poems*, ed. Ian Donaldson (Oxford, 1975), 45. One could argue that this very tension between the conventions of Christian resignation and the immediacy of grief is itself a convention. Such an argument, however, would reduce the poem to merely conventional properties, as though the poem were nothing more than an interplay of conventional elements rather than a dramatization of a perennial human problem. To follow the Ten Commandments would be an admirable way to lead one's life. The problem is how to do it. And this is also a literary problem in that it involves the constant testing of general principles, ideals, or conventions against the circumstantiality of individual life. To say that the tension dramatized in "On My First Son" is also a convention is to forget that Jonson had a son named after him who died in his seventh year. Jonson attempts to reconcile himself to the child's death; he knows he should "loose all father," but the very fact that he has to say this reveals his inability to do it. For a poem in which Jonson does "loose all father," in which his Christian obligations easily overcome his fatherly attachment, see his epigram "On My First Daughter."

12. In the summer of 1972 I visited Cunningham with a friend of mine who had just returned from Europe where he had spent the past year traveling. In the course of telling Cunningham about the places he visited and the things he did, my friend gave a rather animated account of climbing Mount Snowden, how difficult the climb was and how dangerous, but how reaching the top had made it all worthwhile. "It was so beautiful up there," he said, "it was like a religious experience." Cunningham said he could believe that, adding, "I guess I'm just not that hard up for religion."

13. Emily Dickinson, poem no. 822, in *Collected Poems* (Boston, 1952). All further references to this work will be to the poem number and will be included parenthetically in the text.

14. Cunningham, "Quest of the Opal," in *Collected Essays*, 421.

15. See John Baxter, "The Province of the Plain Style," *The Compass* (April 1978): 34.

16. Cunningham, "Journal of Cardan," in *Collected Essays*, 425.

17. See Simone Weil, *Gravity and Grace* (London, 1963), 136.

18. Cunningham, "Ideal Fiction," in *Collected Essays*, 279.

19. Cunningham, "Journal of Cardan," in *Collected Essays*, 426.

20. We can find the same generous attention in Cunningham's criticism; the care he brings to his perception of others in his love poems, he brings to his perception of the text in his essays. For Cunningham, the act of interpreting a text and of respecting another person are analogous. As he says in "The Ancient Quarrel between History and Poetry," in *Collected Essays*, 126:

> The understanding of an author in the scholarly sense involves the exercise under defined conditions of the two fundamental principles of morality in the Western tradition: 1) the principle of dignity, or of responsibility to the external fact, in the special form of respect for another person as revealed in his works; and 2) the principle of love, the exercise of sympathetic insight, or of imaginative transformation. [126]

21. Jonson, "My Picture Left in Scotland," in *Poems*, 26.

22. Alfred North Whitehead, *The Function of Reason* (Boston, 1958), 77.

Some Thoughts on Robert Hass

One of the strengths of Robert Hass' work is his great ability to
describe the world around him. Yet much of his interest in descrip-
tion proceeds from a disturbing desire to live wholly in a world of sen-
sory experience and from a concomitant distrust of intellectuality.
This distrust may seem surprising, as Hass is a plainly intellectual
writer. His poems abound with references to books, films, paintings,
and music: his great temptation is to prefer representations of expe-
rience to experience itself, a temptation for which description serves
as an antidote. Take, for instance, "Spring," a poem from his first
book, *Field Guide*:

> We bought great ornamental oranges,
> Mexican cookies, a fragrant yellow tea.
> Browsed the bookstores. You
> asked mildly, "Bob, who is Ugo Betti?"
> A bearded bird-like man
> (he looked like a Russian priest
> with imperial bearing
> and a black ransacked raincoat)
> turned to us, cleared
> his cultural throat, and
> told us both interminably
> who Ugo Betti was. The slow
> filtering of sun through windows
> glazed to gold the silky hair
> along your arms. Dusk was
> a huge weird phosphorescent beast
> dying slowly out across the bay.
> Our house waited and our books,
> the skinny little soldiers on the shelves.
> After dinner I read one anyway.
> You chanted, "Ugo Betti has no bones,"
> and when I said, "The limits of my language
> are the limits of my world," you laughed.
> We spoke all night in tongues,

in fingertips, in teeth.

The poem turns on the illusion in line five that the "bearded bird-like man" is the answer to the question, who is Ugo Betti. Not until line nine do we realize that he's only someone who can explain who Ugo Betti is. This ambiguity reflects Hass' uneasy sense of culture—which this man embodies—as a kind of secondhand experience. Sensuously forbidding ("priestly") and wearing a raincoat on a sunny day, this explainer is cut off from the physical world, but also metaphorically protected from its weirdness, its evanescence, in part the source of its beauty. The implication is that art not only compensates us for the change on which the brute world is predicated; it is also a prophylactic against sensuality. And Hass indicates the insufficiency of art's compensation by characterizing his books as "skinny little soldiers" opposing the "huge beast" of evening, and by frankly characterizing the man's words about Ugo Betti and his own about language as tiresome, especially when set next to the attractive "slow dying" of the dusk, and the sexual talk that concludes the poem.

The poem shows rhetorical skill: Hass draws the syntax through the free-verse lines expressively, and the contrast between the man and the evening is nicely balanced. But the thinking that animates the poem warrants skepticism: to set sex against reading is like Yeats' specious proposition that one must choose between perfection of the art, or of the life. Devotion to the artifacts of consciousness does not necessarily limit or impair our sensuality. If it did, Paola and Francesa would not have gotten into such hot water.

But this is Hass' difficulty. He is tempted toward an excess of thought, not feeling. It's not surprising that he should warily regard the limitations too much reflection can impose. This awareness, though, too often leads to an equally limiting and formulaic glorification of immediacy, as at the end of "Graveyard at Bolinas":

> The sun was on my neck.
> Some days it's not so hard to say
> the quick pulse of blood
> through living flesh
> is all there is.

"Some days" implies that most days it's damn hard to say there's nothing more permanent or meaningful than the blood's pulse. But this implied struggle is only vaguely gestured at. The speaker gives an amusing account of some of the grave markers ("Eliza Binns is with Christ, which is better"), and some good description. But the details and the humor indicate little of the struggle which the conclusion suggests and from which the poem attempts to draw its power. The hard-earned acceptance and residual resignation implicit in such locutions as "it's not so hard" and "all there is" aren't adequately justified or explained by anything else in the poem. The complexity, in other words, is merely rhetorical.

Hass employs a similar rhetorical strategy (with more success) at the end of "Meditation at Lagunitas," a poem from his second book, *Praise*. The poem, impressive for the terrain it covers in so few lines, has all the provisional feel of an ongoing meditation, of a mind making discoveries as it goes from thought to thought, forcing each proposition toward the exception that informs and qualifies it. Yet Hass' qualifications emerge less from rhetoric than from a desire to keep an honest account as he moves over his subject:

> All the new thinking is about loss.
> In this it resembles all the old thinking.
> The idea, for example, that each particular erases
> the luminous clarity of a general idea. That the clown-
> faced woodpecker probing the dead sculpted trunk
> of that black birch is, by his presence,
> some tragic falling off from a first world
> of undivided light. Or the other notion that,
> because there is in this world no one thing
> to which the bramble of *blackberry* corresponds,
> a word is elegy to what it signifies.

He opens wryly with two examples of "the new thinking": the first derives from the scholastic notion of haecceity—that each particular, by its presence, represents a falling away from a realm of seamless purity, of "undivided light"; the second, also derived from scholasticism, is the nominalist notion that in the representation of the thing the word is, at best, "elegy to what it signifies." What we have then is a double erasure—the general truth erased by each particular, and each particular erased by the word that refers to it.

So far the thinking, abstracted from the particulars of actual experience, has been archly academic, just the kind of thinking Hass indulges in often and consequently so distrusts. What he is really commenting on here is just this tendency in himself toward a rarefied intellectuality, a kind of talking so removed from experience (even when experience is the subject) that the word, indeed, becomes elegy to what it signifies. And he goes on to say:

> . . . After a while I understood that,
> talking this way, everything dissolves: *justice,*
> *pine, hair, woman, you* and *I.*

In moving from the general concept to the particular pronouns, the list of words recapitulates the movement of the whole poem, and it enables him to turn associatively to a personal experience, to rethink the same problems in terms more integral to his life:

> . . . There was a woman
> I made love to and I remembered how, holding
> her small shoulders in my hands sometimes,
> I felt a violent wonder at her presence
> like a thirst for salt, for my childhood river
> . . . .
> . . . It hardly had to do with her.
> Longing, we say, because desire is full
> of endless distances. I must have been the same to her.

Testing the philosophical assumptions about loss against his own experience, he realizes that the woman was in many ways incidental to the associations she evoked. Yet the associations are problematic: what are we to make of "a thirst for salt, for my childhood river"? If she arouses in him a desire to return to some preconscious state, then perhaps these details are related in terms of water: the fresh water of the river, the salt water of the embryonic fluid. "A thirst for salt" may also express a thirst for thirst, a desire for desire (reminiscent of J. V. Cunningham's epigram "How we desire desire"). In either case, this woman arouses in him a longing for some inaccessible state where there are no divisions between word and thing, "you" and "I," and where there is, therefore, no loss. This test-case, then, would seem to support the assumptions on which the poem began. But, determined to prevent these assumptions from simplifying his recollection, he keeps pushing his thought toward the exceptions:

> But I remember so much, the way her hands dismantled
>   bread,
> the thing her father said that hurt her, what
> she dreamed. There are moments when the body is as
>   numinous
> as words, days that are the good flesh continuing.
> Such tenderness, those afternoons and evenings,
> saying *blackberry*, *blackberry*, *blackberry*.

Although the intimate details he now recalls—"the thing her father said," "what she dreamed"—are representations of other experiences, the representations are particular experiences themselves (he makes a similar perception in "The Beginning of September" when he says, "Words are abstract, but *words are abstract* is a dance, car crash, heart's delight"). There are times, he realizes, when the divisions we assume between experience and representations of experience, self and other, word and thing, simply do not matter: instead of longing, which implies distance and privation, at such times the good flesh can continue.

Throughout *Praise*, Hass' distrust, which in his earlier work takes a decidedly anti-intellectual turn, now deepens to become a habit of feeling. What he fears and is now drawn to is desire as longing, as privation. And this, he knows, is not restricted to any one realm of experience. In art, it manifests itself as the desire to sieve out of process some object that will point to a transcendent meaning, to an undivided light: in strictly intellectual matters, it is the desire to escape from the ambiguities and complexities of experience through some single principle or absolute: in love, it is the impossible desire to get out of the self.

Hass now sets as a kind of ideal those experiences associated with "continuing pleasures" rather than epiphanic ones. He seeks to confide in experiences that are larger and more inclusive than the unique occasion. For instance, in "The Beginning of September," it is the mastery of setting the table: "Spoon, knife, folded napkin, fork; glasses all around. The place for the plate is wholly imagined." In "Transparent Garments," in which he rejects the romantic pursuit of darkness (inanimate being) on the one hand, and light (pure spirituality) on the other, he desires to emerge in a nonsymbolic landscape where "the juniper is simply juniper." Likewise, in "Songs to Survive the Summer," the light he's drawn to is terrestrial, it is the light "of all things lustered by the steady thoughtlessness of human use," not the undivided light of "Meditation at Lagunitas"; and in "Santa Lucia," what he or rather what his speaker wants "happens not when the deer freezes," that is, not at the revelatory moment isolated from time, but "when she flicks her ears and starts to feed again," returning to the continuous, normative act.

But continuity is an ideal Hass will have trouble realizing. As he says in "Songs to Survive the Summer," he's caught in the war between "Dailiness and desire," between a craving for the intensity of the climactic moment and an equally strong desire to repose in traditions—continuous, time-honored practices—that embrace more of life than the discrete occasion. This ambivalence produces a curious stylistic mix, tending on the one hand toward a prose inclusiveness, and on the other, within the framework of that inclusiveness, toward a reliance upon the fragment and the list as primary organizing principles. Even when he argues for the continuous and ordinary, as in this prose passage from "The Beginning of September," the argument takes the form of fragmentary impressions:

> Nothing is severed on hot mornings when the deer nibble flowerheads in a simmer of bay leaves. Somewhere in the summer dusk is the sound of children setting the table. . . . The place for the plate is wholly imagined. Mother sits here and father sits there and this is your place and this is mine. A good story compels you like sexual hunger but the pace is more leisurely. And there are always melons.

But these impressions are not traditions. And this impressionistic method pushes the poem toward the very isolation Hass is attempting to reject. It tends toward the unique and isolated occasion, not the normative one which, by definition, depends on recurrence, on the connections between things in addition to the things themselves. In other words, there seems to be an essential disjunction between his method and what he wants that method to accomplish. And it is this disjunction that accounts for the uncertainty and confusion that one meets on almost every page of *Praise*.

A thoughtful and often moving writer, and an immediately appealing one too, Hass is traditional insofar as he is willing to draw upon resources that the past (nonliterary as well as literary) makes available. Works of art, history, philosophy, are joined to personal details in order to make sense of his own experience. And to accommodate this eclectic interest, he has been gravitating toward an inclusive proselike style of composition. But within this style he relies principally on impression and on the juxtaposition of fragmentary details (literary techniques associated with imagist and postimagist practices). And this I think not only limits the effectiveness of his eclecticism, it frustrates and defeats at times the intentions that lead him to a more inclusive style. If he truly desires to bring his art closer to the center of life where "the good flesh continues," he will have to develop a method of composition that is not so inextricably bound up with the intensity of the marginal and momentary, a method that is not, in other words, a kind of formalization of longing itself.

1980

"Itinerary" by James McMichael

The style of James McMichael's poetry has changed from the compressed obliquity of the early work to the loosely shaped meditations of the later. There are genuine accomplishments in both styles yet neither seems entirely successful. In *Against The Falling Evil*, his first book, he shows remarkable talent for image and metaphor, for focusing with intensity on the resonant detail; and in a few poems such as "The Assassin" and "The Vegetables," he manages through the obliquity of metaphor to treat serious subjects with precision and depth of feeling. Yet cumulatively, despite the varied array of surfaces, the early poems all begin to sound alike, as if they had been generated by the tight-lipped style itself, not by anything he has to say. Furthermore, unlike his neighbors there—Strand, Merwin, James Tate, Gregory Orr, William Mathews and Charles Wright—McMichael was only passing through, not settling down. But if the early poems seem too restricted, his recent autobiographical work, *Four Good Things*, seems too unrestrained. This is not to deny that there are passages of exceptional quality in the poem. But the leisurely discursive pace, the unemphatic meter, the breadth of detail, and the flexibility with respect to tone and diction are driven to such excess that the poem loses a discernible principle of exclusion. Like Mount St. Helens, it keeps erupting, but often all we see is ash.

His other long historical narrative, "Itinerary," from his second book, *The Lover's Familiar*, is not only his best poem but is, I think, one of the best poems by any American poet in the postwar period. Unlike *Four Good Things*, it establishes a firm prosodic structure which exerts enough pressure on the syntax to keep the prose virtues from dissipating into mere prose. This metrical control provides him with a rhythm that can respond sensitively to changes in feeling and perception. For instance, in the closing passage when the speaker reaches his greatest understanding of experience, McMichael indicates this emotional and intellectual elevation by shifting from the four-beat accentual norm into traditional blank verse. The naturalness of this rhythmical transition reinforces the sense that the closing experience has emerged naturally from all that has gone before. In contrast, because the prosodic structure is looser and less defined in

Four Good Things, variations of rhythm coincident with variations of feeling and perception are difficult to locate, if not altogether absent.

"Itinerary" also establishes a more clearly articulated narrative structure which, in addition to the prosodic one, further controls the seemingly casual movement of the syntax. The poem moves eastward across America and backward in time, beginning with the poet in the Far West and ending with an eighteenth-century New England Puritan walking in his garden. Speaker succeeds speaker as gradually as one landscape emerges from another, each one conveying a deepening experience of the natural world that spans the strict reportorial, the scientific, the mercantile, the religious, and, underlying all of these, the erotic. Here are the opening lines:

> The farmhouses north of Driggs,
> silos for miles along the road saying
> Butler and Sioux. The light saying
> rain coming on, the wind not up yet,
> animals waiting as the front hits
> everything on the high flats, hailstones
> bouncing like rabbits under the sage.
> Each runnel mixing where it can,
> the spring creeks deepen and go on
> easily, swelling to the larger
> tributary with its pools and banks.

The first involvement between the poet and the landscape is ironically the most detached. Our subjugation of the continent culminates in the West; yet this subjugation has resulted in such spiritual estrangement that, in mastering the physical world, we have eliminated from it all meaning but the utilitarian. We have had to demystify nature, dissolving all sense of its sacredness, in order to exploit it. Now the silos simply say Sioux, a purely nominal survival of a people once in harmony with the environment; the light saying only rain is purely phenomenal, carrying no suggestion, as it later will, of the divine. The flood of participial phrases and the syntactic fragments create an overwhelming sense of so much going on that the speaker can only observe and list without comprehending, in the radical sense of the word. This is a landscape of pure happening, in other words, of things without ideas in them.

For many recent poets, this perception of flux would be the only legitimate view of reality; for McMichael, though, it is just provisional. Consider, for instance, how the last four lines do more than simply describe. The expansive movement from runnels to spring creeks to larger tributaries prefigures physically what each successive speaker will experience spiritually as we journey toward the garden; the landscape, without sacrificing any literal accuracy, is already implicitly metaphoric for some spiritual potential within the poet, but it is a potential that, speaking in his own voice and time, he cannot realize. Only by projecting himself backward into history can he re-collect and revive that connection between himself and the world and at the same time understand how it came to be broken. (This sort of figurative description is, of course, very traditional, though it has been largely discontinued since Frost; that McMichael should revive it here suggests that the spiritual resuscitation in the poem will be also literary).

As we move across the continent, more and more eroticism enters into each speaker's perception of the land. Early in the poem, the speaker, probably Meriwether Lewis, regards the great plains in exclusively scientific terms, matter-of-factly describing the "indifferent" soil ("indifferent" suggesting the erotic in a dormant state), restricting his interest in the river to its "weight," "altitude," and "gravity." A little later, another speaker notices with clinical detachment that the oppossum "can draw the slit so close that one must look / narrowly to find it if she be virgin." And still further on someone else describes with patent randiness the Indian women "whose most negligent postures reveal / nothing to our curiosity." At the same time, the poem becomes increasingly more violent. In fact, there are places where the violent and the sensual seem indistinguishable, as in the lines describing how rattlesnakes take a squirrel: "They ogle the poor beast til by force of charm / it falls down stupefied and senseless." The one quality serves to normalize or balance the other, so if the perception of violence restrains the desire to "seek congress with the earth" by showing that "it sings its lovesongs for no man," the erotic in turn prevents the speaker from seeing only violence.

This sense of balance becomes even more apparent in the juxtaposition of two later passages. In the first, the speaker, William Bird, after drinking river water ("what Adam had in paradise") says that "our slumbers sweeten. / And if ever we dream of women they are kind." Yet in the very next lines he observes that the myrtle plant, though sacred to Venus, "grows commonly in dirty soil." Whereas earlier in the poem the river water is regarded from an exclusively sci-

entific point of view, the water here assumes the power of an aphro-
disiac. Likewise, as we move into the voice of the final speaker, the
New England Puritan, in whom the erotic merges with the religious,
we get another, more spiritual version of the myrtle plant, of the
sacredness that grows in dirty soil:

> There have been divers days together
> wherein alone I've watched these flowers
> buoyed on their stems and holding up the sun.
> Just now I catch them thinking on themselves,
> composing from their dark places the least
> passages for light, tendering how they look
> and how I look on them.

To lessening degrees as we approach the garden, meaning accrues to
things unilaterally from the mind; but it now resides within things so
thoroughly that nature becomes more symbolic than real. This is why
these flowers, unlike all other plant life in the poem, are neither liter-
ally described nor named, for the flow of significance now comes from
them: "tendering how they look / and how I look on them." Just as
these flowers bring all four elements together ("buoyed" suggesting
water and air, "sun" suggesting fire, and "stem" of course suggesting
the earth to which they are rooted), so they offer the speaker a vision
of experience in which this spiritual orientation ("holding up the
sun") depends on the earthly fact of being rooted. Likewise, when
they open, "thinking on themselves, / composing from their dark
places the least / passages for light," they suggest an image of the self
opening to God, composing out of its moral darkness a passage for the
light of grace. And perhaps it is not too much to suggest that they also
tender an image of poetic composition at its most inclusive, in which
opening out to the world and turning in to the self become comple-
mentary movements of a single activity.

In coming upon these flowers, McMichael's speaker is given a
vision of fullness bordering on beatitude. Yet what animates the
entire passage is the clear-sighted, complex understanding of the
world that he demonstrates even in his most beatific moment. If he
experiences grace here, the grace shows itself not as mystical forget-
ting or mindless unity, but as realization that elevates consciousness
to a height from which the earthly considerations that have dominat-
ed the poem up to now, the dark places in the self and nature, are not

left behind so much as comprehended:

> It comes to me
> that the world is to the end of it
> thinking on itself and how its parts
> gather with one another for their time.
>
> These are the light, and all the forms they show
> are lords of inns wherein the soul takes rest.
> If I could find it in myself to hide
> the world within the world, then there would be
> no place to which I could remove it, save
> that place wherein all things come to see.

When McMichael characterizes the forms of light as lords of inns, he is in effect acknowledging that even the rest his soul now takes is only temporary lodging, a lucid interlude on a journey that, as the entire poem shows, is fraught with violence, uncertainty, and restlessness. Moreover, when one realizes that the speaker is in fact preparing for the journey that the poem has already recorded, and that the conclusion represents a kind of hopeful prayer, one archaic meaning of the word "itinerary"—a prayer for safe passage made at the beginning of a journey—comes alive. And this revivification in turn further qualifies the speaker's state of grace, suggesting that he implicitly anticipates the dangers that we, as readers, know he will encounter.

What we reach then is a state of comprehension, a fullness of response to the world that includes fear, joy, an awareness of evil, of time, even of the fragility of the comprehension itself. We reach a state of mind, in other words, that can recognize important similarities between the self and nature along with equally important differences, and that can maintain, if only within the privileged sanctuary of the garden, a precarious balance between "promiscuous wonder" on the one hand, and knowledge of "ill terms" on the other.

What makes "Itinerary" so remarkable is partly the way its historical materials are so assimilated by the poet's sensiblity that they become the medium for intensely personal realizations, and partly the way that, in amassing, brooding on, and making sense of those materials, McMichael remains committed to the whole of consciousness, attempting to discover within the self among its various faculties, and between the self and its historical as well as personal circumstances, its past as well as present, that balance that will afford access to fullness. If, as Nathaniel Hawthorne once remarked, happiness is the capacity to live throughout the whole range of one's faculties and sensibilities, then "Itinerary" is a happy poem, despite the troubling nature of so much of what it says.

1980

The Liberal Imagination of Robert Pinsky's *Explanation of America*

At the end of "Tennis," a poem from his first book, *Sadness and Happiness*, Robert Pinsky implies that he would like to write a kind of poetry that seeks to "understand the world, and all its parts." The two halves of this phrase (pressed apart by the comma) not only suggest the ambitious and unfashionable range of his poetic interests, they also highlight a tension at the center of the poetry he actually writes: between the desire to understand the world in general, and the often conflicting desire to understand or embrace the world in all its various, irreducible parts. The first desire leads to a discursive poetry of principles and definitions; the second, by referring always back to the concrete world of contingent parts, fosters a distrust of principles and definitions. These divided aspirations make him push his verse with Jesuitical rigor toward the particular exceptions, the circumstances that complicate and sometimes undermine entirely his desire to generalize. Pinsky is compelled to explain like a philosophical realist while at the same time assuming a nominalist's distrust of explanation. This is why his rhetorical posture is so often tentative and exploratory, why he is attracted to the longer forms where his dialectical habit can be fully exercised, and why stylistically he relies on syntactic qualifiers and adversatives the way so many of his contemporaries rely on images, similes, and metaphors.

In *An Explanation of America*, his book-length poem to his daughter, we can see the virtues and limitations of his dialectical, self-questioning style. In the broadest terms, the book takes up the same tension between the desire for certain knowledge and the recognition that "Countries and people of course / Cannot be known in final terms . . . / But can be, in the comic halting way / Of parents, explained." "Halting" aptly describes his stopping and turning method at its best and worst. On the one hand, it enables him to deal liberally with each experience, to approach his subject by any avenue—image or idea, principle or circumstance, type or particular—and to move, however haltingly, toward some provisional judgment that can clarify the conflicting details and attitudes that he confronts. At its worst, though, it leads him into a kind of emotional and intellectual paralysis, what one might call a liberal's (bittersweet) stupefaction before his own ambivalence, before "the plural-headed Empire, manifold / Beyond my outrage or my admiration." His best and worst tendencies are illustrated respectively in "A Love of Death" and "Bad Dreams," poems which appear sequentially in section two of *An Explanation of America*, "Its Great Emptiness."

In "A Love of Death" Pinsky addresses a subject he treats exhaustively in *The Situation of Poetry*: the romantic and modern poets' "nostalgia for inert being, which for the mind is death." This nostalgia stems from a profound uneasiness with consciousness itself, with the distance it inevitable places between the self and nature. Since the romantic period, the desire to bring the mind closer to the natural world has been a central literary preoccupation. But inasmuch as every act of writing is an act of consciousness, the romantic poet must, as Pinsky remarks in his fine chapter on Keats' "Nightingale," regard "the natural world nostalgically across a gulf that can be crossed only by dying, either actually or through some induced oblivion." The poem approaches this subject indirectly at first, through a recreation of two scenes from Willa Cather's novel, *My Antonia*. It is illuminating to compare Cather's prose passage with Pinsky's blank-verse adaptation, for though he remains faithful to the original text in detail, his few changes are revealing. In the novel, the narrator is recollecting a personal childhood experience of oceanic oneness:

> I sat down in the middle of the garden, where snakes could scarcely approach unseen, and leaned my back against a warm yellow pumpkin. There were some ground-cherry bushes growing along the furrows, full of fruit. . . . All about me giant grasshoppers, twice as big as any I had seen, were doing acrobatic feats among the dried vines. . . . There in the sheltered drawbottom the wind did not blow very hard, but I could hear it singing its humming tune up on the level, and I could see the tall grasses wave. The earth was warm under me, and warm as I crumbled it through my fingers. . . . I was something that lay under the sun and felt it, like the pumpkins, and I did not want to be anything more. I was entirely happy. Perhaps we feel like that when we die and become a part of something entire, whether it is sun and air, or goodness and

knowledge. At any rate, that is happiness; to be dis-
solved into something complete and great.

Here is Pinsky's version of this scene:

> Or, imagine the child in a draw that holds a garden
> Cupped from the limitless motion of the prairie,
> Head resting against a pumpkin, in evening sun.
> Ground-cherry bushes grow along the furrows,
> The fruit red under its papery, moth-shaped sheath.
> Grasshoppers tumble among the vines, as large
> As dragons in the crumbs of pale dry earth.
> The ground is warm to the child's cheek, and the wind
> Is a humming sound in the grass above the draw,
> Rippling the shadows of the red-green blades.
> The bubble of the child's heart melts a little,
> Because the quiet of that air and earth
> Is like the shadow of a peaceful death—
> Limitless and potential, a kind of space
> Where one dissolves to become a part of something
> Entire . . . whether of sun and air, or goodness
> And knowledge, it does not matter to the child.
>
> Dissolved among the particles of the garden
> Or into the motion of the grass and air,
> Imagine the child happy to be a thing.

Pinsky takes a more complicated attitude toward this experience than
Cather's narrator, balancing between caution on the one hand, and
wistful admiration of the other. The caution is particularly evident in
the few places where his version deviates from the original. For
instance, it is evening in his poem, thereby associating the experience
with the coming on of darkness and, metaphorically, with death, but
morning in Cather's novel; and where her grasshoppers are compared
to acrobats, his are seen as more threatening dragons. His image of
the child's heart melting like a bubble makes explicit what is implicit
in the prose: that in the limitless expanse of the prairie, human iden-
tity seems utterly fragile, limited, and insignificant. The cautionary
tone rings clear in the repetition of the word "child," which occurs
five times in the lines above, and ten times in the entire poem. In one

sense, along with the muted iambic cadence this repetition heightens
the hypnotic beauty of the experience. But it also reminds or even
warns that this Edenic harmony is possible only for a child. Because
the child's identity is still essentially unformed, he can entertain as a
benign possibility becoming "part of something entire." He can be
happy to be a thing because for him the sun and air, goodness and
knowledge are interchangeable. The speaker admires this ("Imagine
the child happy to be a thing"), longs for it, yet understands that such
happiness can have only menacing consequences for an adult:

> Imagine, then, that on that same wide prairie
> Some people are threshing in the terrible heat
> With horses and machines, cutting bands
> And shoveling amid the clatter of the threshers,
> The chaff in prickly clouds and the naked sun
> Burning as if it could set the chaff on fire.
>
> . . . .
>   A man,
> A tramp, comes laboring across the stubble
> Like a mirage against that blank horizon,
> Laboring in his torn shoes toward the tall
> Mirage-like images of the tilted threshers
> Clattering in the heat. Because the Swedes
> Or Germans have no beer, or else because
> They cannot speak his language properly,
> Or for some reason one cannot imagine,
> The man climbs up on a thresher and cuts bands
> A minute or two, then waves to one of the people,
> A young girl or a child, and jumps head-first
> Into the sucking mouth of the machine,
> Where he is wedged and beat and cut to pieces—
> While the people shout and run in the clouds of chaff,
> Like lost mirages on the pelt of prairie.

Unlike the Edenic childhood garden, the prairie is an alien force with
which these immigrants exist in conflict, not agreement. The warm
ground of the earlier passage becomes a terrible heat, just as the
peaceful quiet turns into the clatter of the threshers. This is the fall-
en world of adult consciousness. Yet against the "pure potential" of
the "pure blank spaces" human life appears miragelike for all its suf-

fering and labor, a trick of the mind. And in a sense it is, for it is the mind that makes us conscious of our limitations, of ourselves as separate from our surroundings and not part of anything entire. Insofar as oneness and awareness are mutually exclusive states, we are denied the dissolution into nature that the child can happily experience. This is why, perhaps, the tramp, the adult version of the child, jumps "head-first" into the thresher. But Pinsky finally insists that one cannot really say why, because the tramp in his action has left explanations far behind.

Pinsky then imagines the kind of poetry one might write, desiring this entire strangeness, this pure potential of the quiet plain:

> Imagine that a man, who had seen a prairie,
> Should write a poem about a Dark or Shadow
> That seemed to be both his, and the prairie's—as if
> The shadow proved that he was not a man,
> But something that lived in quiet, like the grass.
> Imagine that the man who writes that poem,
> Stunned by the loneliness of that wild pelt,
> Should prove to himself that he was like a shadow
> Or like an animal living in the dark.
>
> In the dark proof he finds in his poem, the man
> Might come to think of himself as the very prairie,
> The sod itself, not lonely, and immune to death.

Merwin and Strand are the most famous Shadow Poets of our time: attempting to pierce the false screens that the mind erects between the self and reality, their work moves through an unconscious, darker region where the self, to quote from Strand, "no longer belonging to me" is "asleep in a stranger's shadow." But the self achieves this undifferentiated harmony, this immunity to death, at the expense of life itself; in desiring to become the sod, one discards a world that one can know and talk about in favor of a world where one can only be. Pinsky clearly rejects this desire. Yet what gives this poem as a whole such power is his willingness and capacity to present this desire sympathetically without hedging his judgment of it. The attraction does not undermine or erode the judgment so much as suggest the sense of cost involved in making it.

In "Bad Dreams," however, the judgment does falter as Pinsky

explores the implications this thirst for pure potential has for other
nonliterary contexts. At its most general level, this thirst expresses a
profound dissatisfaction with actual life. Yet as so much actual life is
objectively in need of change, not acquiescence, it is involved in the
formation of political and moral aspirations, and in the ambiguities of
living "always in vision":

> People who must, like immigrants or nomads,
> Live always in imaginary places
> Think of some past or word to fill a blank—
> The encampment at the Pole or at the Summit;
> Comanches in Los Angeles; the Jews
> Of Russia or Roumania, who lived
> In Israel before it was a place or thought,
> But a pure, memorized word which they knew better
> Than their own hands.
>
> And at the best such
> people,
> However desperate, have a lightness of heart
> That comes to the mind alert among its reasons,
> A sense of the arbitrariness of the senses:
> Blank snow subordinate to the textbook North.
> Like tribesmen living in a real place,
> With their games, jokes or gossip, a love of skill
> And commerce, they keep from loving the blank of death.
>
> But there are perils in living always in vision—
> Always inventing entire whatever paves
> Or animates the innocent sand or snow
> Of a mere locale.

Pinsky acknowledges that people who must live in imaginary places
can, like the Jews in the diaspora imagining Israel, subordinate "the
actual snow to the textbook North," the oppressive circumstance to
the idea or purpose. "The mind alert among its reasons" has a kind
of freedom or detachment from even unbearable circumstances and
can thereby keep from loving the blank of death. But he realizes that
there are also dangers implicit in having to "invent entire whatever
paves / Or animates the innocent sand or snow / Of a mere locale."
The key word here is "entire," which associates this kind of visionary

detachment with the romantic poet's love of death, of being part of something entire. The implication is that an obsession with an abstract goal or with pure particularity or process—with the "mystic home" or with the sod—amounts to the same thing, for in either case life is drastically simplified. Both the exotic and the ordinary offer the self a release from the vagaries of circumstance, from the tensions of individual consciousness and moral choice:

> A man who eats the lotus of his prairie
> Or shadow—consumed by his desire for darkness
> Till the mind seems itself a dreamy marrow—
> Is like those creatures of a traveler's nightmare.
> Even his sentiments about the deer,
> Or grass, recall man-eating Polyphemus:
> . . . .
>   In place of settled customs,
> Such a man might set up a brazen calf,
> Or join a movement, fanatical, to spite
> The spirit of assembly, or of words—
> To drown that chatter and gossip, and become
> Sure, like machines and animals and the earth.

Pinsky wants us to see that the vices or perils of living always in vision are closely tied to its virtues. Though vision provides some detachment from contingency and some control over it, it can also lead to or proceed from a desire to be free of contingency altogether, to lose oneself *entirely* in something. The Jews who live the admirable nomadic life, "who have," to quote Nietzsche, "that freedom of mind and soul which mankind learns from frequent changes of place," are also the ones who, perhaps in reaction to the tensions which that freedom creates, set up the brazen calf. Likewise, the Cyclops who Pinsky fears may one day lumber through his daughter's life finds its counterpoint in the figure of Brutus who appears in a later poem about aspiration: "And who can say / What Brutus may come sweeping through your twenties?" Brutus is a more attractive fanatic, but a fanatic nonetheless. His love of death differs from the Cyclops' or the romantic poet's in that his expresses not a nightmarish rejection of life's possibilities so much as a heroic validation of values that the Roman Republic had betrayed. All the same, Pinsky still describes him as "half-mystical, wholly romantic," implying, it seems, that every great act is in some

sense a fanatical one, that there is a Polyphemus in every Brutus, and
that there are times when the two are indistinguishable. But the ques-
tion Pinsky raises in an earlier poem and which "Bad Dreams"
attempts to answer remains unanswered: "Living inside a prison /
Within its many other prisons, what / Should one aspire to be?" In
some sense every act of freedom "within the accumulating prison of
the past / that pulls us toward a body and a place" represents a resis-
tance to the gravity of historical circumstance, even as it is condi-
tioned by that circumstance. But at what point does that resistance
become a desire to escape from life entirely into some mystical home?
Or conversely, at what point does accepting the limitations of circum-
stance, the settled customs of a place, become complacency and resig-
nation? Considering the importance of the question, Pinsky's answer
seems disappointingly pat:

> What I want
> And want for you is not a mystic home
> But something—if it must be imaginary—
> Chosen from life, and useful.
> . . . .
> Americans, we choose to see ourselves
> As here, yet not here—as if a Roman
> In mid-Rome should inquire the way to Rome.
> Like Jews or Indians, roving on the plains
> Of places taken from us, or imagined,
> We accumulate the customs, music, words
> Of different climates, neighbors and oppressors,
> Making encampment in the sand or snow.

What he wants is not the mystic home outside of time and place, but
(like Robert Hass) some continuous interaction among imagination,
life, and place: an encampment, a temporary resting place in the
snow. America, being a place of rapid change, becomes a metaphor
for this encampment. It is a place where we can choose to see our-
selves as on the one hand fixed and continuous (here), and on the
other evolving toward some visionary goal (not yet here). In this
respect we are like the nomadic Jews, attached and unattached to cir-
cumstance, neither given over to the mere locale like the hypothetical
romantic poet in his nostalgia for the sod (Pinsky shows that the actu-
al Keats was not so naive), nor detached from it like the Protestant

settler in his pursuit of a mystic home.

Yet this only brings us back to square one. For the nomadic Jew slips easily into the one who establishes the brazen calf of immanence. Pinsky shifts from one type of visionary to another, lumping together Jews, fascists, romantic poets, protestants, and cyclopes without much historical elucidation, as if they all represented some single tendency, or were conditioned by one historical cause. He never explains really what this cause is; nor does he explain how or why the one kind of visionary worthy of admiration is pressed by historical circumstances into the one we ought to fear. If he's saying that all these types, these bad dreams, embody versions of some deep desire to simplify life to wholly manageable proportions, he's really saying very little; one could charge, in fact, that Pinsky is committing the very act of simplification that he seems to censor.

But perhaps this is just to say that Pinsky's enormous capacity to move intellectually and emotionally around his subject—one of his most attractive qualities—can sometimes get the better of him. When he is successful, as he so often is, he manages to express an acute sense of the "manifold" nature of things without at the same time abandoning "outrage" or "admiration," or the need for principles and values, however circumscribed or provisional. But when the subject seems too multifarious, as it does in certain sections of *An Explanation of America*, his liberal, discursive manner covers a lot of ground without getting anywhere; at such times, for all his heuristic intentions, Pinsky seems as evasive and noncommittal as the ironic or imagistic poets he describes so well in *The Situation of Poetry*.

All in all, he is an important poet. Without excluding the images and documentary details that have become the standard fare of so much recent verse, he manages to traffic in ideas with honesty, humor, and intelligence. Moreover, his inclusive yet controlled habit of composition is not only a much needed corrective to practices that have tended to displace poetry to the margins of life, it establishes him—despite the conventional appearance of his work—as one of the more daring and experimental poets of his generation.

1980

"a living to fail":
The Case of John Berryman

By imputing none of his miseries to himself, he continued to act upon the same principles, and to follow the same path; was never made wiser by his sufferings, nor preserved by one misfortune from falling into another. He proceeded throughout his life to tread the same steps on the same circle.
—Samuel Johnson, *Life of Savage*

He hugged his sorrow like a plot of land,
And walked like an assassin through the town,
And looked at men and did not like them,
But trembled if one passed him with a frown.
—W. H. Auden, "The Bard"

In an interview two years before he killed himself, John Berryman described the lucky artist as one "who is presented with the worst possible ordeal that will not actually kill him. . . . What happens in my poetic work in the future will probably largely depend . . . on being knocked in the face and thrown flat, and given cancer. . . . I hope to be nearly crucified." By these standards, Berryman was lucky right from the start. His father committed suicide when he was twelve; his mother was a domineering and possessive woman from whose disruptive influence he was to suffer throughout his life. Manic-depressive and suicidal himself, by his mid-thirties he was an alcoholic and a drug abuser, and this, together with his compulsive womanizing, drove him through two marriages and nearly destroyed a third, turning his life into a monotonous round of crisis, breakdown, and hospitalization. By the age of fifty, with the publication of *77 Dream Songs*, he was nationally recognized as one of the most distinguished poets of his generation; yet even recognition became another source of pain, one more ordeal to suffer through, causing him to worry over his prestige and reputation like a sweaty broker at the stock exchange.

The myth of the tragic artist, whose unhappiness is the inevitable price he pays for artistic power, was an article of faith for the poets of Berryman's generation. As Lowell wrote in his elegy for Berryman, "we had the same life / the generic one / our generation offered." Lowell himself, Theodore Roethke, Dylan Thomas, Delmore Schwartz, and even at times Randall Jarrell all lived disordered lives; to varying degrees they regarded marital chaos, alcoholism, and suicidal despair as occupational hazards and found in each other's suffering a terrible sanction for their own. Of course, the assumption that pathology and inspiration, art and suffering, are somehow related did not originate with them but is as old as western civilization. Since the Romantic period especially, it has troubled and preoccupied every generation of poets. But to see the latest mutation of this idea we need only compare Wordsworth's version with Berryman's.

The poet, as Wordsworth defines him in the preface to the *Lyrical Ballads*, differs from other men only in degree, not kind, and this difference resides in what he calls "a greater promptness to think and feel without immediate external excitements, and a greater power of expressing such thoughts and feelings." The poet's mind is so primed, so heightened naturally, that it does not require, as less heightened minds do, "the application of gross and violent stimulants." This power, moreover, lies not in any special kind of experience (for his experiences are essentially the same as other men's), but rather in his intensity of recollection and his skill of expression. However, Wordsworth does believe that poets often live unhappy lives, for if by virtue of their heightened sensibility they derive more pleasure from ordinary experience, they also derive more pain. Although poets may be more tempted by the satisfaction of their appetites, and this may get them into trouble, Wordsworth never equates trouble with inspiration or artistic skill.

In Berryman's view, on the other hand, "this greater promptness to think and feel" is dependent on, even addicted to, "external excitements." His thinking is tightly circular and goes something like this: as a poet, I'm entitled to indulge in all temptations because they make me feel more alive and thereby stimulate my creative energies; but these indulgences also make me suffer because, being more sensitive than others, I feel extraordinarily guilty; yet suffering is a good not only because it gives me something to write about, but because it also justifies the painkiller of more self-indulgence. Thus, Berryman not only confuses excitement with inspiration, he confuses pleasure with pain, especially in *The Dream Songs*, where he continually draws connections between trauma (whether in the form of womanizing, drugs, or emotional catastrophe) and poetry: "Hunger was constitutional" with Henry, "women, cigarettes, liquor, need need need / until he went to pieces. / The pieces sat up & wrote" (311); "Feeling no pain, / Henry stabbed his arm and wrote a letter" (74); "They are shooting me full of sings" (54). So also in Dream Song 26, he treats poetry and adultery as analogous expressions of criminal behavior in being examples of uncontrollable appetite:

> The Glories of the world struck me, made me aria, once.
> —What happen then, Mr Bones?
> if be you cares to say.
> —Henry. Henry became interested in women's bodies,
> his loins were & were the   scene of stupendous achievement.
> Stupor. Knees, dear. Pray.
>
> All the knobs & softnesses of, my God,
> the ducking & trouble it swarm on Henry,
> at one time.
> —What happen then, Mr Bones?
> you seems excited-like.
> Fell Henry back   into the original crime: art, rime
>
> besides a sense of others, my God, my God,
> and a jealousy for the honour (alive) of his country,
> what can get more odd?
> and discontent with the thriving gangs & pride.
> —What happen then, Mr Bones?
> —I had a most marvellous   piece of luck. I died.

The glories of the world struck Henry: they impressed him or seduced him, yes, but they also injured him (perhaps as by a slap in the face). Aria can also be taken two ways: on the one hand, the world provides Henry with an aria, it sings to him and so draws him, siren-like, into experience; but on the other hand the world makes Henry sing an aria and so transforms him into a poet: "What happen then, Mr Bones? . . . Henry." Aesthetic appetite ("Henry became interested in women's bodies"), sexual excitement ("his loins were & were the scene of stupendous achievement"), fears of sexual failure ("Stupor. Knees, dear. Pray"), and the ducking, trouble, and guilt give way to the original crime of poetry, which in turn gives way to the desire for fame and an obsession with the thriving gangs of rival poets. Poetry is the original crime in so far as (like original sin) it is, for Berryman, an inherited disposition which precedes experience and determines the kind of experience one has. Adultery is really just the sexual expression of the poet's artistic needs. It serves those needs by stimulating his imagination and providing it with subject matter. His life, in other words, is merely fodder for his poetry.

The Dream Songs, along with Lowell's *Life Studies*, have been praised for breaking from what is often called "the fifties poem," a poem of highly wrought aesthetic surfaces, disciplined, polished, learned, and complex in tone and language, and obliquely related, if at all, to personal experience. As A. Alvarez describes it in *The Savage God*, this overly refined, overly sophisticated poetry could take "no account of the confusions and depressions of a life unredeemed by art." The direct autobiographical style of *The Dream Songs* represents an effort to "push . . . at the limits of what poetry can be made to bear," to invite into the domain of art "the tentative, flowing, continually improvised balance of life itself." Yet what emerges from a close reading of *The Dream Songs*, and from John Haffenden's four-hundred-page biography of Berryman, is a portrait of an artist who held mere life in contempt, for whom life had no intrinsic worth except insofar as art could validate it. Since great art demanded, in Berryman's words, "gigantic, unspeakable but articulate disaster," Berryman arranged his circumstances so that he would be bound to suffer. As Haffenden puts it, he resolved "to adopt the mantle of the suffering life, to live intensively and to use his life as discipline. . . . in arrogating to himself fundamental exercises in tragic art, he was in a way courting disaster in his personal life." Berryman himself described these aspirations in a poem written on his twenty-second birthday:

> What breaks about my head next year or next
> Let it be intolerable, let it be
> Agony's discipline, let it not be strange.

Such ideas are anything but strange in a twenty-two-year-old poet. When "agony's discipline" is only an imagined, not a real, experience, it is easy to romanticize. The strangeness is that Berryman would adhere so tenaciously to this adolescent program and continue throughout his life to rationalize his own pain and the pain he caused others by claiming they were indispensable conditions of his art. So in 1950 he confides to his journal, "My decision last week . . . was not to worry so but to take fucks when they turned up . . . perhaps that is not an abominable programme *if it lets me work whereas I otherwise wouldn't*" (italics his); likewise, in 1953 he writes to his mother, "Where the rage comes from I don't altogether understand, though I know a good deal about it and I think it may be an unavoidable concomitant of a certain kind of intolerable painful, exalted creation. Any artist not a saint, that is, who loves humanity as much, while torturing himself as much, as I did and was during parts of the composition of the poem, with that intensity over a protracted time, may be bound to take it out on humanity (any specimens that are unlucky enough to be by) afterward." The "unlucky specimen" he refers to here happened to be his wife. Older, though no wiser, in a 1962 interview, thinking of himself, he says of Mozart, "His whole life was at the mercy of his art. It is incredible. I'm thinking of that and I'm also thinking about the kind of hysterical states that modern artists go in very much for—an extreme case would be Van Gogh's cutting off his ear—periods of masochism and blasphemy—that kind of business . . ." Compulsive as he surely was, early and late Berryman was nonetheless a very "businesslike" manipulator of experience; even at his most destructive, he assumed, in Haffenden's words again, "the aspect of spectator of his own drama" and measured the value of each experience in terms of the poetry it might produce.

Perhaps the most outrageous example of this specialized mentality (though the biography is full of them) is the infamous "Lise Affair." In the summer of 1947 Berryman became involved with the wife of a Princeton graduate student. It was during this affair that he started drinking heavily; not surprisingly, the excitement of the affair inspired a manic outpouring of sonnets—over a hundred in a two-month period. In the journal which he kept during this period he excused his infidelity by claiming, "my will has been at the service of my passion and my imagination." An Aeolian harp played by erotic impulse and inspiration alike, he used the same language to describe his passion for Lise that he often used to describe the poems he was writing. As Haffenden observes, he often commenced writing sonnets "helplessly," that many were "unexpected," that he couldn't "stop writing," that they "go on," and that he was surprised to find "I have eleven sonnets planned." At other times the language of obsession and hysteria ("All upside down, mad, guilty and frightening") alternated with the language of the cool, self-conscious artist, paring his fingernails as he falls apart: "Isn't my ideal of style at present: what will be lucid and elegant, but also surprising, frightening and various?" In the sonnets themselves, this detachment takes the form of identifications with past adulterers and sonneteers—Bathsheba's David, Sidney, Petrarch, Balzac—identifications which cast an immortal literary glamour around his personal chaos. So when the affair ended, despite the damage it did to his marriage and despite how much Lise made him suffer, he could look back gratefully: "I owe her, besides times and days of unspeakable happiness: 1) the sonnets, though I abhor them just now, 2) a knowledge of women extraordinary and new, 3) a deterioration in my nervous state . . . which now looks to draw me out of much *more* pain than Lise made me herself and older difficulty." How quickly Berryman slid over the mention of "unspeakable happiness" in order to get to the poems and the pain! And more pain, of course, meant more poems. Why else have an affair? In her memoir *Poets in Their Youth*, Eileen Simpson, Berryman's wife at the time, offers the same motive:

> As for John, was it Lise he wanted? Or the sonnets
> Lise inspired, as Yeats had been inspired by Maud
> Gonne? "If Miss Gonne had called Willie's bluff and
> gone to bed with him, she wouldn't have filled his days
> with misery. No misery, no poems. You can bet your
> life that what Yeats was after was the poems," John
> used to say when asked what he made of their rela-
> tionship. Was a new subject for poems what he too
> was after?

To suggest, as Berryman and Simpson do, that Yeats deliberately cultivated what he bitterly called, in "Pardon, Old Fathers," "a barren passion" for Maud Gonne, that he preferred misery to fulfillment for the sake of the poetry that misery would generate, is to simplify self-servingly Yeats' life and work. It is, furthermore, to forget that Yeats wrote only minor poetry during the unhappy period of his love for Maud Gonne, and that his greatest poetry came only after he had married Georgie Hyde-Lees and finally achieved a state of marital contentment and stability. As Richard Ellman points out, "Had Yeats died instead of marrying in 1917, he would have been remembered as a remarkable minor poet. . . . If bachelorhood had continued, we may reasonably assume also that personal problems would have gone on operating as they had done for many years, as brakes upon his mind. Marriage to Georgie Hyde-Lees released his energies like a spring." Or as Yeats himself put it in a letter written eighteen years before his marriage, "I think that a poet . . . becomes a greater power from understanding all the great primary emotions & these one only gets out of going through the common experiences & duties of life." Berryman's correspondence then, "No misery, no poems," reduces the rich and complex figure of Yeats into a mirror within which Berryman could find a justifying precedent for all the wayward aspects of his personal life.

Similarly, throughout *The Dream Songs*, Berryman identifies himself with artists and cultural heroes in order to explain his suffering or justify his self-indulgence:

> Scarlatti spurts his wit across my brain,
> so too does *Figaro*: so much for art
> after the centuries yes
> who had for all their pains above all pain
> & who brought to their work a broken heart . . .
>
> —Dream Song 258

> Churchill was ever-active & crammed with glee,
> Henry was morbid, inactive, & a child to Angst,
> there the difference ends.
> They both drank, heavily.
> . . . .
>   Both wrote things down,
> both thought on their feet,
> and both spent the bulk of their long lives out of favour:
> . . . .
> disabling their achievement: . . .
>
> —Dream Song 323

Yet Berryman is also the master poet of the guilty conscience, tormented by an unrelenting and indefinable sense of sin:

> But never did Henry, as he thought he did,
> end anyone and hacks her body up
> and hide the pieces, where they may be found.
> He knows: he went over everyone, & nobody's missing.

. . . .
Nobody is ever missing.

—Dream Song 29

But such self-loathing is often merely self-exaltation in disguise. As an
Artist in the Modern World, Henry is a kind of Everyman. His
heightened sensibility compels him to respond so fully, so intensely, to
the world that he comes to embody, in all aspects of his experience,
the spirit of his age. This yoking together of public and private expe-
rience is, according to A. Alvarez, the crucial feature of the extremist
poetry that Berryman and Lowell wrote, a poetry in which "the
nihilism and destructiveness of the self . . . turns out to be an accurate
reflection of the nihilism of our own violent societies." By identifying
Henry with criminals (mass murderers, Nazis, corrupt politicians) to
illustrate his violence and rage, or with Jews and blacks to illustrate
the intensity of his suffering, Berryman gives Henry "a ruin-prone
proud national / mind" (Dream Song 77) and thereby tries to turn his
personal experience, good and bad, as victim and victimizer, into an
internalized expression of his culture:

> 'All virtues enter into this world:')
> A Buddhist, doused in the street, serenely burned.
> The Secretary of State for War,
> winking it over, screwed a redhaired whore.
> Monsignor Capovilla mourned. What a week.
> A journalism doggy took a leak
>
> against absconding coon ('but take one virtue,
> without which a man can hardly hold his own')
> the sun in the willow
> shivers itself & shakes itself green-yellow
> (Abba Pimen groaned, over the telephone,
> when asked what that was:)
>
> How feel a fellow then when he arrive
> in fame but lost? but affable, top-shelf.
> Quelle sad semaine.
> He hardly know his selving. ('that a man')

Henry grew hot, got laid, felt bad, survived
('should always reproach himself'.

—Dream Song 66

Henry's representative significance, however, is nothing more than a
rhetorical effort of the penultimate line in which Henry's experience
joins together by mere association the disparate experiences which
the poem addresses: Henry is like the Buddhist by growing hot, the
Secretary of State by getting laid, the monsignor by feeling bad, and
the absconding coon by surviving.

   Throughout this essay I treat Henry and Berryman as inter-
changeable, and some readers may object to this. After all, Berryman
did dissociate himself from Henry in the introductory note to *The
Dream Songs*, calling him "an imaginary character (not the poet, not
me)." And insofar as Henry speaks in vaudevillian dialects, in rhyme
and meter, and has experiences Berryman couldn't possibly have had
(at one point he even dies and comes back to life), this is obviously
true. On the other hand, if Henry is only an imaginary character (not
the poet, not Berryman), how is it that he has the same friends and
relatives, the same vices, the same obsessions—not to mention the
same profession? And why did Berryman occasionally refer to him-
self as Henry in letters and conversation? The fact is Berryman want-
ed it both ways, for Henry is really his ventriloquist's dummy,
through whom he could speak directly of himself and at the same time
evade complete responsibility for what he says. It's precisely Henry's
exaggerated mannerisms, his obviousness as a persona, that legit-
imizes, as it were, even the most intimate disclosures, the most puffed-
up and egocentric attitudes. So in poems like Dream Song 66, Berry-
man can imply through Henry a causal link between his inner
disarray and national disorder, or arrogate the suffering of blacks to
dramatize his own unhappiness, and still deflect the charge of self-
indulgence. But such poems *are* self-indulgent, however cagily Berry-
man throws his voice, and for this reason: the experiential authority
that would justify the self-inflated claims is only asserted through a
trick of style, not dramatized or discovered within the detailed ten-
sions of private life.

   But compare Dream Song 66 with Dream Song 191, a poem in
which Berryman does persuasively and movingly elicit general signif-
icance from his own experience. The poem is about old age and the

death of friends, and the manner is unusually plain with little of the tricks and fripperies that dominate the Dream Song style. It is a manner appropriate to the quiet, yet deeply troubled, meditation on surviving those one loves, of living to an age when one's very consciousness becomes "a house of death":

> The autumn breeze was light & bright. A small bird
> flew in the back door and the beagle got it
> (half-beagle) on the second try.
> My wife kills fleas & feeds them to the dog,
> five last night, plus one Rufus snapped herself.
> This is a house of death
>
> and one of Henry's oldest friends was killed,
> It came on a friend' radio, this week,
> whereat Henry wept.
> All those deaths keep Henry pale & ill
> and unable to sail through the autumn world & weak,
> a disadvantage of surviving.
>
> The leaves fall, lives fall, every little while
> you can count with stirring love on a new loss
> & an emptier place.
> The style is black jade at all seasons, the style
> is burning leaves and a shelving of moss
> over each planted face.

Despite the plainness, the poem is intricately structured: as Berryman moves toward the elegiac language of the closing lines, he unobtrusively changes from the blank verse of the first stanza, to the partial rhymes of the second, to the full rhymes of the third. Likewise, as the relatively trivial details of animal death give way in the second stanza to the death of "one of Henry's oldest friends," Berryman switches from the first-person pronoun to the third; by means of this he distances the sorrow from himself, but the distance itself intensifies rather than dilutes that sorrow, suggesting that his sense of loss is so acute that he can articulate it only by turning the part of himself that feels it into Henry. Yet Henry, too, disappears in the last stanza, generalized into the second person "you," just as his grief is generalized into a style of "black jade at all seasons," a style necessitated by the "disadvantage of surviving."   There are traces of the Dream Song manner in the juxtaposition of "leaves" and "lives" and in the pun on "burning leaves," but the manner is subdued even at such moments, and remains throughout a sensitive response to the occasion it presents. The general meaning, moreover, rises through the particular biographical details, instead of being, as in so many of the Dream Songs, merely an effect of style, or an assertion.

But this is a rare exception. For the most part, the assumption that his experience is intrinsically significant or representative allows Berryman merely to indulge in all the petty, egotistical worriments of daily life: ("Henry as a landlord made his eight friends laugh / but Henry laughed not: the little scraggly-bearded jerk / has not paid his rent for two months" (336); "Your first day in Dublin is your worst. / I just found my fly open: panic!" (299); "Trunks & empedimenta. My manuscript won't go / in my huge Spanish briefcase, some into a bag" (332). The same assumption also allows him to seem a harsh judge of himself, but it's only an apparent harshness, because his judgments invariably shade off into indictments of the world that ultimately made him what he is: "What the world to Henry / did will not bear thought" (74); "Baseball, & the utter fucking bloody news, / converged on miserable Henry" (197).

In the same interview I quoted at the beginning of this essay, Berryman describes more explicitly why modern artists are destined to lead such dreadful lives:

> You ask me why my generation seems so screwed up?
> . . . it seems that they have every right to be disturbed.
> The current American society would drive anybody
> out of his skull, anybody who is at all responsive; it's
> almost unbearable. . . .   From public officials we
> expect to get lies, and we get them in profusion. . . .
> Perhaps Sylvia Plath did the necessary thing by
> putting her head in the oven, having to live with those
> lies.

This is bardolatry at its purest. No one would deny that we are products of culture or that our individual neuroses have social and political as well as psychological causes. But in Berryman's life and work this conflation of public and private experience, and the related assumption that the poet risks his life in order to confront the repressed truth about himself and his society, amounted to an evasion of responsibility: Instead of drawing from his personal history the sympathy that would take him imaginatively into the experience of other sufferers, Berryman merely arrogated the credentials of other sufferers, in order to invest his own despair with special dignity and confer upon himself a kind of privileged immunity from social norms. Living the life he thought high art required, he believed he could redeem and ennoble everything he did, however base or brutal, by virtue of the poetry he wrote.

Yet Berryman is praised for being almost Christ-like in his devotion to disaster. As Joel Conarroe puts it: "Artists like Berryman . . . who live perilously close to the abyss make it possible for us to journey over threatening terrain, to experience its terror and to return intact. . . . In courting certain kinds of disaster, Henry spares us the necessity of doing so ourselves, overpowering as the attractions sometimes are." In this view, Berryman surrenders to the impulses the rest of us repress so that we can feel the terror of the abyss without the danger, and thereby be spared from following his example. He drinks himself into a stupor, sleeps around, and destroys his marriage, and so saves us from the same temptations. This shamanistic view of the poet is as naive as Berryman's self-serving belief that trauma in all its forms is an indisputable sign of artistic election. Even had he treated his addictions as addictions, not as a muse, I doubt that *The Dream Songs* could keep anyone seriously tempted by disaster from going mad, or drinking heavily, or cheating on his or her spouse. But those who are not seriously tempted by disaster—only trivially so—can read *The Dream Songs* and be titillated or, worse, feel justified in their prurient fantasies. Reading for them becomes a form of armchair debauchery whereby they can convince themselves that their temptations, however mild or ordinary, make them compellingly human, even poetic, without their suffering any of the consequences of "the poetic life."

In the conclusion to *Poets in Their Youth*, Eileen Simpson refuses to blame Berryman's suicide on his having been a poet. Though "the litany of suicides [among poets] is long . . . it was the poetry that had kept him alive . . . that he died a 'veteran of life' was thanks to his gift. . . . Only when there were no more [poems] did he feel . . . that 'it seems to be DARK all the time.'" This may seem at first like a sane corrective to the confessional cant that Berryman and his critics spout, but in effect it's no less horrifying. For it rests serenely on the assumption that a poet's exclusive source of value is his poetry, that his life is "at the mercy of his art." If, as Simpson claims, poetry kept Berryman alive, his idea of poetry ratified the kind of life he led, a life that could have ended only in suicide. His assumptions about the poet and his relation to the world may not have caused his appetite for self-destructive drama, but they did encourage it.

And the same ideas which exacted and excused the imperfections of the life also encouraged the imperfections of the work. Since poetry alone could validate his existence, he erected a conception of the poet that would enable him to write at will, and to mistake an aesthetics of suffering for an articulation of the underlying structures of suffering, the personal conflicts at its source. The tortured syntax, the punning and neologisms, the black-face dialect, the mingling of profane and sacred language coincident with the manic fluctuations of self-mockery and self-exaltation—these are merely the rhetorical effects of pain. Granted, the rhetoric is almost always impressive; moreover, there are poems in *The Dream Songs* that redeem the victimized buffoonery from mere mannerism, or that work by sheer force of verbal ingenuity, despite the highly mannered surface. That Berryman managed to write well at all is remarkable given the extent and seriousness of his suffering. In assessing his work, however, we should not confuse, as he did, his suffering with his poetic gifts, dissolving the complex powers of aesthetic realization into a set of pat experiences. If ordeal were the most important ingredient of artistic achievement (especially the particular ordeals which Berryman was prone to), our detox centers and mental hospitals would be full of artists. No one but God perhaps can say whether Berryman would have written better had he lived and thought differently. But one thing is certain: however much his talent may have thrived on trauma, trauma in turn confined his talent to a narrow range of experience which he believed to be the most profound because the most extreme.

But the extreme in style as well as content is at best a marginal position. If poets are exemplars of consciousness, then our greatest poets should be those who exercise the widest range of faculties upon the widest range of life. Against this standard, Berryman can be regarded not as a representative man whose self-destruction was a badge of authenticity or of deep responsiveness to an irredeemably corrupt society, but rather as a brilliant eccentric. Instead of bringing or attempting to bring the whole soul into activity, he was compelled, like Savage, to tread the same steps on the same circle. And as an artist, his circle is finally too small and too mannered. And no one would want to make a model of the life.

1983

Part 4

The Dead Alive and Busy

I've been teaching poetry at the university level for eight years, and it never ceases to disappoint me that the poems I have greatest difficulty teaching are the ones I care the most about. In the classroom there's nothing more discouraging than seeing what you regard as a rich account of what it means to be alive reduced to a dry academic exercise discussed, by teacher as well as student, as though it had been written to be interpreted by a class. This is, I suppose, what makes teaching a challenging profession—the hope that somehow you can transcend the academic setting and show how poetry can extend one's sympathies and deepen one's vision of the world. In most cases this hope is doomed to disappointment. The great poems in our language can intensify our awareness, but they presuppose, in order to do so, a level of prior awareness many students don't possess, given their age and circumstances. It's not that most students are too inexperienced to appreciate the emotional sophistication of, say, Hardy's poems of 1912–13. Everyone by the age of nineteen or twenty has more experience than years of psychotherapy could accommodate. It's rather that they're unaware of the experiences they have had, and unaware partly because they have no genuine sense of their mortality; unconsciously, most young students think they'll live forever. And this is a natural function of their age, health, material well-being (at least at the universities where I have taught), and beyond this, of living in a culture in which death is largely an abstraction, confined as it is to the hospital and isolated from the home. Without a genuine sensitivity to change and the fragility of life, undergraduates won't appreciate the best poems as deeply as you would like them to. So you talk about technique, structure, history, patterns of influence, and hope that they'll discover at some later time, when they've grown more aware of their own experience, that good poetry can help them clarify and understand their lives. It's one of the strange aspects of teaching (as sad as it can be heartening) that you are seldom ever present when what you teach bears fruit.

But there are a few occasions when it is otherwise. The most memorable one for me occurred in a course I taught at Stanford University several years ago on the history of the lyric poem. Among the twenty or so junior and senior English majors and graduate students in the class, there was one freshman, a girl named Patty Smith. Normally freshmen are discouraged from enrolling in upper level courses, but a colleague and friend of mine, Nora Cain, with whom Patty had studied poetry writing in the fall, had highly recommended her. Nora told me that Patty had recently been sick with cancer, though the disease was at the moment in remission. Nora insisted that Patty didn't at all require special consideration, and that she was one of the brightest and most serious students Nora had ever taught and was eminently capable of holding her own against students with more formal training.

It so happened that the majority of poems we were reading had to do with various aspects of personal and cultural loss. And it was clear from the first week of class that what were mere assignments for the majority of students were matters of life and death for Patty. This is not to say she was a self-indulgent reader, or that she ever talked about herself in class or in her papers. She was the soul of reticence. More than any student I have ever known, she paid meticulous attention to what she read; she tried to understand each poem in as much detail as possible, as though her troubles had instilled in her a passion for accuracy, had intensified her concentration and made reading well a psychological necessity. For instance, during the first week of class we discussed a poem called "Meditation 8" by Philip Pain:

> Scarce do I pass a day, but that I hear
> Some one or other's dead, and to my ear
> Me thinks it is no news. But oh! did I
> Think deeply on it, what it is to die,
>   My pulses all would beat, I should not be
>   Drowned in this deluge of security.

I talked about the way Pain distinguishes a knowledge that others die, something one knows only in the mind ("and to my ear / Me thinks it is no news"), from the emotional as well as mental *realization* that he himself will die ("My pulses all would beat"), and I tried to show how this turn from knowledge to realization is supported by the slightly disturbed rhythms of lines four and six, and by the instability of the concluding rhyme. The class itself discussed the interesting figurative reversal in the last line, of drowning in security. But it was Patty who

pointed out that the realization doesn't actually occur, it's only enter-
tained hypothetically. The speaker doesn't say his pulses all beat
when he imagines dying, only that they would beat if he did imagine
dying. "The thought of his own death is so frightening," she said,
"that he can only imagine himself imagining what it is to die. He can't
get any closer."

The other poem I remember Patty responding deeply to in the
first week of class was "The Oxen" by Thomas Hardy:

> Christmas Eve, and twelve of the clock.
> "Now they are all on their knees,"
> An elder said as we sat in a flock
> By the embers in hearthside ease.
>
> We pictured the meek mild creatures where
> They dwelt in their strawy pen,
> Nor did it occur to one of us there
> To doubt they were kneeling then.
>
> So fair a fancy few would weave
> In these years! Yet, I feel,
> If someone said on Christmas Eve,
> "Come; see the oxen kneel,
>
> "In the lonely barton by yonder coomb
> Our childhood used to know,"
> I should go with him in the gloom,
> Hoping it might be so.

Patty had two perceptions about this poem. When another student
characterized the speaker's transition from remembered childhood
innocence and faith to adult skepticism, Patty added that what's
interesting about the skepticism is that it's expressed in terms of a
longing to believe. She could understand, she said, someone not hav-
ing faith, but she couldn't understand someone not wanting faith.
She also noticed how as a child the speaker was content merely to pic-
ture the oxen kneeling in the barton, but how as an adult he imagines
himself needing to go outside to check. Even the hopeful adult, in
other words, requires empirical evidence whereas the child takes on
faith what he is told.

No one would describe these poems as uplifting or consoling in what they say. Yet I think they offered consolation to Patty not just by reflecting and clarifying what she must have felt at times, but also by breaking the solitude such feelings create. Hence the poems that consoled her most weren't necessarily the most optimistic or affirmative. What she needed, to use Kenneth Burke's terms, were poems that named her situation realistically. Patty would have perfectly understood Burke's notion of literature as "equipment for living," as strategies for dealing with experience: Great literature, he says, "singles out a pattern of experience that is sufficiently often *mutandis mutatis*, for people to 'need a word for it' and to adopt an attitude towards it." And this demands of course unflinching clarity: "One must *size things up* properly. One cannot accurately know how things *will be*, what is promising and what is menacing, unless he accurately knows how things *are*." I think Patty was compelled by her illness to find accurate names for the psychological situation her illness induced. And this was why she read with such urgent care.

Oddly enough, the poet who engaged her most was Wallace Stevens. Stevens is often described as a poet's poet, quintessentially modern in his lifelong preoccupation with the aesthetic process, with the relationship between imagination and reality, expressed with a style full of gorgeous nonsense, in which the exotic and dandified often mingle with the abstract and philosophical,

> . . . in bright excellence adorned, crested
> With every prodigal, familiar fire,
> And unfamiliar escapades: whirroos
> And scintillant sizzlings such as children like,
> Vested in the serious folds of majesty. . . .

Stevens is so much an aesthetic specialist, making poetry itself the subject of so many of his poems, that there is hardly any indication in his work that he had ever married, fathered a child, entertained his friends, and worked in an insurance firm for most of his adult life. Though one could argue that there's just as great an absence of biographical detail in Pound or Eliot, and that their work is as remote from ordinary life, one still feels, much more than in Stevens, the personal and social tensions which stand back of their allusive or symbolic landscapes; *The Waste Land*, for instance, is as much about the breakup of a marriage as it is about the breakup of a cultural tradi-

tion. Neither Eliot nor Pound, moreover, would have told Robert
Frost, as Stevens is reported to have told him, "The trouble with you,
Frost, is that your poetry has subjects."

This hardly tells us why a dying eighteen-year-old girl would be so
fascinated by his work. Yet there's another way of characterizing
Stevens' principal concerns that I think helps explain her fascination.
In *The Necessary Angel*, Stevens defines poetic truth as "an agree-
ment with reality, brought about by the imagination of a man disposed
to be strongly influenced by his imagination, which he believes, for a
time, to be true. . . . " By agreement he simply means an experience
of harmony between the self and world. Yet the key phrase here is
"for a time," for reality is seen in terms of constant change, and these
agreements with it can be only momentary. By means of these imag-
ined agreements, though, as J. V. Cunningham observes, Stevens
achieves "some intuition of permanence in the experience of absolute-
ness, though this be illusory and transitory, something to satisfy the
deeply engrained longings of his religious feeling." The problem, in
other words, which he explores in poem after poem, is the desire for
stability, or peace with his surroundings, in an ephemeral world. In
this light one can understand why Patty—made painfully aware of the
ephemerality of things—would have a special sympathy for Stevens'
work.

The clearest and most poignant expression of this longing for per-
manence is "Sunday Morning." And it was "Sunday Morning" that
inspired Patty's most interesting and passionate responses. She had
no trouble seeing how Stevens' emotional attachment to a religious
tradition he intellectually rejects is reflected in the dialogue-like
movement between the speaker and his female persona, the woman in
effect being a kind of projection of that part of his nature still nostal-
gic for the "imperishable bliss" of the Christian afterlife. She men-
tioned that the poem is in a way a somber, more elaborate version of
the carpe diem motif of Marvel's "To His Coy Mistress," which we had
discussed the week before. "Sunday Morning" appealed to her more,
she said, because of the more serious occasion and because the affir-
mation of the temporal world and sensory experience doesn't ignore
or play down the realities of loss. In this sense she found the affirma-
tion, "Death is the mother of beauty," similar to the closing couplet of
Shakespeare's sonnet 73:

This thou perceiv'st, which makes thy love more strong,

To love that well which thou must leave ere long.

Taking this cue from Patty, the class worked through the poem
stanza by stanza, reconstructing the implicit steps by which Stevens
reaches his conclusion: since desire itself implies change, insofar as it
entails moving from a state of wanting to a state of having, to a state of
having had; and since change implies loss, and loss implies death—
therefore "Death is the mother of beauty." I should say here that this
is the kind of paraphrase I resorted to when the class had difficulty
following the movement of imagination which the poem dramatizes.
What I tried to make the students see in the sequence of images and
details were the various ways change and loss complicate even as they
enhance the woman's perception of the natural world: the evanes-
cence of beauty intensifies her desires and compels her to find "in
comforts of the sun, / In pungent fruit and bright, green wings . . .
Things to be cherished like the thought of heaven," but the perception
of evanescence also deepens her need for "some imperishable bliss."
    Then we reached the stanza in which Stevens portrays heaven as
a boring, artificial refuge from change: nothing is lost in heaven
because nothing can change there; yet by the same token, since noth-
ing changes, nothing can be enjoyed:

> Is there no change of death in paradise?
> Does ripe fruit never fall? Or do the boughs
> Hang always heavy in that perfect sky,
> Unchanging, yet so like our perishing earth,
> With rivers like our own that seek for seas
> They never find, the same receding shores
> That never touch with inarticulate pang?
> Why set the pear upon those river-banks
> Or spice the shores with odors of the plum?
> Alas, that they should wear our colors there,
> The silken weavings of our afternoons,
> And pick the strings of our insipid lutes!
> Death is the mother of beauty, mystical,
> Within whose burning bosom we devise
> Our earthly mothers waiting, sleeplessly.

But Patty quarreled with this stanza. She said she found it rhetori-
cally heavy-handed in that Stevens presents one particular vision of

paradise as the only possible one. "But there are other ways of imagining heaven," she said. "Heaven could be a place where there's change without loss, though in this world that's difficult to imagine." When I asked her to elaborate, she came up with a musical analogy: "When we listen to a piece of music, each note disappears into the next as soon as we hear it. But, in heaven each note would go on playing; change there would be addition, not subtraction, as it is here." She went on to say that if Stevens had allowed the woman to be a more formidable opponent she might have countered his vision with this one. Yet even here she could see that Stevens betrays a deep attachment to the idea of an afterlife. His rejection is by no means simple or unequivocal. How else interpret the plaintive cry—"Alas, that they should wear our colors there"—except as meaning, why are we still compelled to project an eternal world in which the pleasures change makes possible (the fruit which only time can ripen, "the silken weavings of our afternoons") are dissociated from the losses change inevitably entails? The plaintive tone belies how deeply ingrained our need for imperishable bliss is; it tacitly acknowledges how difficult it is to find any deep or lasting consolation in a mutable world.

This, Patty said, was why she loved the poem, despite her quarrel with it, and why she found the last stanza, in particular, so moving, especially in the way it shows how indivisible are beauty and evanescence, and in the way the affirmation of the last phrase, "on extended wings," is qualified and yet required by the darkness into which the pigeons sink:

> She hears, upon that water without sound,
> A voice that cries, "The tomb in Palestine
> Is not the porch of spirits lingering.
> It is the grave of Jesus, where he lay."
> We live in an old chaos of the sun,
> Or old dependency of day and night,
> Or island solitude, unsponsored, free,
> Of that wide water, inescapable.
> Deer walk upon our mountains, and the quail
> Whistle about us their spontaneous cries;
> Sweet berries ripen in the wilderness;
> And, in the isolation of the sky,
> At evening, casual flocks of pigeons make
> Ambiguous undulations as they sink,

Downward to darkness, on extended wings.

It occurs to me that there are many bad or undistinguished poems that express essentially the same ideas, that exhort us to seize the day and make the full life our response to the fact of death. Would these poems have solaced Patty? Would they have elicited from her as much perception? I don't think so, and for this reason: such poems fail insofar as they fail to recreate stylistically, in the formal tactics of expression, the vital apprehension of the physical world they advocate. Moreover, in so far as stylistic mastery is the formal extension of emotional and intellectual intensity, we can speculate that "Sunday Morning" would have meant more to Patty than lesser poems on the same theme because it comprehends more, because it attains, in Burke's words, "*a full moral act* by attaining a perspective *atop all the conflicts of attitude*," a perspective which the particulars of style reflect.

2

The cancer returned shortly after the winter quarter; by July Patty was dead. Since then I've taught "Sunday Morning" countless times at Northwestern University, where I now teach. Last year a student in one of my classes came from Patty's hometown and was a friend of her younger sister Sandy. She told Sandy I had mentioned Patty in class, and Sandy in turn told her parents, who then wrote to me asking for details of the story. They also sent along a manuscript of Patty's poetry in which this poem appears, untitled:

> The memory of drugged and pain-filled hours
> Adds urgency to every sunlit day
> When I, frantic, gather loads of flowers
> Only to watch the bright blooms fade away.
> The thought of death turns normal days divine,
> Sweetens every kiss and conversation.
> I want to make each waking moment mine
> And close my eyes with haunted hesitation.
> Still, sleep alone dissolves away the pain,
> I dream for days in dizzy whirls of grey
> And stumble from my nauseous stupor sane

Yet aching for the hours drugged away.

I mourn for life too beautiful to leave;
Thank God I have so much for which to grieve.

Despite the routine phrasing and the poeticisms here and there, the poem is moving and complex, especially the closing couplet. Clearly one can see the influence of Stevens and Shakespeare. And yet the poem is as much indebted to her own experience as it is to her reading. It is as much a young girl's attempt to face her own mortality as it is an act of literary homage. Teachers, myself included, have a tendency at times to talk as though all poems were merely the product of other poems, existing in some precious isolation from the world. But all great art faces two ways. It looks as deeply out into the world as it looks back into its own literary past. And in looking out it strives after an idealized reconstitution of experience—attempting to present, to quote from Burke again, "in a 'pure' or consistent manner some situation which, as it appears among the contingencies of real life, is less effectively coordinated; the idealization is the elimination of irrelevancies." Poetic form is an essential element in this idealizing process; it provides a technique of refinement by which one may distinguish relevant from irrelevant details, ideas or perceptions, and thereby clarify some situation or experience. It shouldn't seem odd, then, that a young girl dying of cancer would express herself in a Shakespearean sonnet, for the sonnet is a gift of sorts from the literary past, an expressive resource discovered and refined by poets long dead, enabling Patty to make sense of the difficulties of her life. Her poem is the conjunction of her responses as a reader with her experience as a mortal human being.

Let me revise somewhat my opening comments. Perhaps we can say that there are two kinds of poems—poems that wake you up, and, on a higher level, poems that assume you're already awake so they can wake you even more. These categories aren't necessarily exclusive; not all poems can be indisputably identified as one kind or the other. Yet in the first group I think we could include certain imagist poems that attempt to strip from perception the deadening film of habit and convention. Williams' "Red Wheelbarrow" or "The Lily" would be examples of this type of poem. "Richard Cory" would be another. We might even include in this group poems by Stevens in his flamboyant, hocus-pocus manner, in which he tries to show through those exotic quirky surfaces the fiction-ridden nature of language. But a poem like "Sunday Morning" I'd place in the other camp. For it requires a measure of awareness in order to be deeply understood. If Patty's illness had awakened her beyond her years, "Sunday Morning" in turn enabled her to experience partly as opportunity what someone else might have experienced wholly as occasion for despair. Poems like "Sunday Morning" and sonnet 73 were gifts to a dying girl, and her poem in return is a kind of gratitude. I think in this light of Henry Vaughan's great poem, "To His Books," and his wonderful phrase for the act of reading as "the dead *alive* and *busie.*" Stevens and Shakespeare are very much alive in Patty's sonnet, intimately conversing with a young girl on the dangers and opportunities of being mortal.

3

I don't know what conclusions to draw from Patty's example. I certainly don't think one needs to be dying of cancer in order to read well. Such experience could easily have the opposite effect and compel one to read his or her own obsessions and preoccupations into the text. I'm not offering a kind of *lecteur maudit* theory of reading whereby the reader requires himself to suffer cancer or divorce or alcoholism before he can appreciate the poet's work. And yet I think the *lecteur maudit* is an exaggeration of a truth which Patty illustrates and which we sometimes lose sight of in the classroom. Perhaps there's a distinction to be made between usable and exploitable experience. Just as the *poète maudit* exploits his life, inviting catastrophe for inspiration, so also the *lecteur maudit* exploits his by making his problems an excuse for reading self-indulgently, for reducing the text into a mirror that gives back only what he wants to see and not necessarily what's there. Our particular experience and temperament, for instance, may predispose us to interpret a man hurrying into a waiting car as a bank robber, or businessman late for an appointment with his shrink, or any number of possibilities which closer examination and thought would corroborate or refute. The good reader would use his own life when reading, would draw on it as a basis of sympathy, but also go beyond it if he had to. Good reading issues in self-knowledge but not only by identification or appropriation, but also by enabling the reader to find expression for what he or she already felt but could not articulate. Because the feeling or idea was unarticulated, it remained unknown to its possessor, till the poem released it.

If all great art is symbolic of a kind of moral plenitude, of conflicting attitudes and impulses explored and worked through toward some ideal clarity, the act of reading is itself a model of ideal human relations, aspiring toward a perfect attentiveness in which emotional possession and intellectual comprehension—what experience conditions us to see and what the text insists we see —inform and alter one another. Reading well, in other words, is symbolic loving. If most students, still too naive to integrate their own experience into their conception of themselves and others, haven't yet discovered this, perhaps we can prepare them for this discovery by cultivating an intelligent enthusiasm for the poems that attempt to wake them, and when we can, for the poems that assume they are already awake.

1984

Horace and the Reformation
of Creative Writing

1

The most frustrating silence in the history of Western literature occurs in the fourth canto of the *Inferno* when Virgil introduces Dante to four of the great poets of antiquity—Homer, Horace, Ovid, and Lucan. After the poets welcome Dante into their company, they all walk on through Limbo together, "talking of things," Dante tells us, "it is well to pass in silence, even as it was well to speak of them there."[1]

What do the poets speak of there on the outskirts of hell? And why does Dante coyly call attention to a conversation he refuses to relate?

Stylistic propriety alone can't account for his mysterious silence since throughout the poem he often digresses from his story to discuss all manner of things with the souls he meets. Here as elsewhere in the *Inferno*, geography, the circle to which the souls have been assigned, provides the better part of judgment so that Dante himself is free to exercise a wider range of attitudes to the stories he is told, and to the souls that tell them. In this particular case, it enables him to respond to these poets as poets, not as pagans, however virtuous. And these aren't just any poets either, but the most illustrious masters of the tradition Dante himself was schooled in and is now preserving and extending in the very poem he is setting out to write. These are his poetic mentors, in other words, those who have prepared him to make the journey he is now embarked upon. In this respect the meeting in Limbo can be seen as a metaphor for the peculiar combination of arrogance and humility that all poets cultivate in relation to the achievements of their predecessors: humility that acknowledges the need for teachers, for models of excellence, and arrogance that insists on one's capacity to learn. Thus Dante honors his teachers precisely by taking his place among them, after Virgil, "sixth amid so much wisdom." [2]

So why then is he as reticent about that conversation as he is proud to tell us that it occurred?

It's as if the poets talking together constitute a secret society absorbed within yet still distinct from the Christian universe's strict economy of sin and redemption. To think of these poets as forming a secret society may seem at first to contradict the traditional view of them as cultural educators, addressing not a specialized audience of other poets but the community itself, or the ruling class of that community, embodying and preserving its moral and spiritual ideals. Yet just as art, even the most culturally inclusive, is Janus-faced, looking out toward the experiential world and in toward the conventions that select, arrange, shape, and so transform that world into formal meaning, so also poets have always regarded poetry in a dual light: as a highly specialized skill or techne governed by its own particular norms and conventions, and as a divinely or irrationally inspired medium for the preservation and transmission of cultural value.

We can think in this connection of the master bards or Ollaves of pre-Christian Ireland. To become an Ollave and assume the role of cultural curator, or public memory, the poet had to pass through a very rigorous twelve-year course of training, encompassing not only the study of prosody and the memorization of all the tales and poems of the nation, but also, among other things, the mastery of history, music, law, science, and divination. His was a poetry inextricably bound up with the realities of social and political life. And yet as Robert Graves points out, the bard "knew the history and mythic value of every word he used and can have cared nothing for the ordinary man's appreciation of his work; he valued only the judgment of his colleagues, whom he seldom met without a lively exchange of poetic wit in extempore verse." Part of his training, moreover, involved the mastery of "one hundred and fifty Oghams, or verbal ciphers, which allowed him to converse with his fellow poets over the heads of unlearned bystanders."[3] Perhaps the silence in which Dante shrouds his conversation with the master poets of antiquity is a kind of ogham, allowing them to talk shop, so to speak, over the head of the general Christian reader. If so, given that these were Dante's predecessors in the genres of epic and satire, as in so much else, an important part of their discussion would, I imagine, have to do with the education of the poet, and with the doctrine of imitation that formed (from antiquity through the late eighteenth century) the cornerstone of a poet's training in his art.

2

One would think American poets have a particular interest in eaves-
dropping on the conversation of the master poets of the past since in
the modern world America is the only culture to have institutionalized
the teaching of creative writing. The sheer number of MFA programs
in creative writing—over two hundred at last count—ought to testify
to a general belief in the classical ideal of poetry as a learned profes-
sion, in literary expertise as the mastery of all the traditional
resources of the art, and in imitation of past accomplishment as the
means by which such mastery is achieved.

Yet the ideas and practices that inform the education we provide
our writers, which in turn informs the way they write, derive in large
part from an Americanized translation and reduction of certain
essentially romantic tensions between imagination and intellect, ener-
gy and order, organic process and mechanical rule. In the European
romantic tradition poetry (and art in general) was primarily seen as
an integrative and reconciling force among the various opposing fac-
ulties within the self, and between the self and nature. American
romanticism, on the other hand, is deeply informed by the puritan
tradition that preceded it and against which it in part defined itself.
One essential aspect of this tradition was the moral and intellectual
tendency to divide all experience into mutually exclusive categories:
for the puritan this meant, of course, saint and sinner, good and evil,
election and damnation, predestination and will, and so on. An Amer-
ican romantic such as Emerson inherits the exclusive and puritanical
habit of mind but replaces the puritan's moral oppositions with those
inherited from Coleridge, Wordsworth, and certain late eighteenth-
century German philosophers. In the Emersonian transvaluation of
values, the morally severe dichotomies of saint and sinner, or good
and evil, are converted into the softer distinction of the supremely
valuable (imagination, impulse, and nature) and the basically neces-
sary but not sufficient in itself (intellect, will, and convention).

The ghost of that puritanical severity, however, has haunted and
still haunts the way American poets have handled these distinctions,
predisposing them to turn what for the romantics were mutually
entailing (if not easily reconciled) ingredients into implacable opposi-
tions. This was especially apparent in the rhetoric that surrounded
the experimental poetry of the sixties and seventies: "good" became
quite explicitly synonymous with imagination, irrationality, and

impulse; and "evil" with all forms of metrical and moral control. And poetry, instead of struggling to reconcile antithetical needs and appetites, came to be identified exclusively with the "good" half of the opposing terms, with one set of human faculties. In the eighties, that severity in turn produced, among many of the poets associated with New Formalism, an equally severe reaction that merely perpetuated the same exclusive thinking in reverse: now "good" became synonymous with metrical control, and "evil" with the irrational energies that free verse sanctioned.

As they are currently set up, creative writing programs are the pedagogical equivalent of this exclusive thinking. The opposition of imagination and intellect, for instance, finds its institutional extension in the separation of creative writing from the more discursive genres of essay and criticism; likewise the opposition of predetermined rule and process accounts for the virtual disappearance of any serious study of the prosodic past in favor of the more organic rhythms of free verse, which are often described in the vague terms of music, ear, and intuition and are therefore not amenable to systematic analysis.

This raises another point. The study of prosody is guild knowledge. The secret societies that formed the bardic colleges of ancient Ireland and Wales were based primarily though not exclusively upon technical expertise. Our contemporary version with its rhetoric of intuition and organicism has led ironically to a kind of guildlike promotion of technique, but one based on terms too muzzily defined to be anything more than a mystifying "je ne sais quoi" sensitivity. Which is to say, attention to technical matters dissociated from a historical understanding of how the techniques themselves evolved has led to another sort of secret society in which vagueness and mystification pass for knowledge.

Most writing programs are founded on the paradoxical assumption, as described by the Iowa Workshop's statement of purpose, that "writing cannot be taught but that writers can be encouraged."[4] In this view, education involves not the assimilation of a traditional body of knowledge or a set of practices but the discovery and cultivation of individual sensibility, personal vision, or "voice." Learning to write becomes a mode of self-discovery, or as Marvin Bell puts it, a process whereby students "begin to accept what they are and to actually work with what they are and to build on that. Now this is what I would like to encourage in my students."[5] If learning to write means, to quote

another creative writing instructor, "moving towards one's own voice
and one's own speech and one's own rhythms," then it follows that no
general curriculum required of everyone can be established.[6] Or as
the statement of purpose for the writing program at Washington Uni-
versity says, "since no two writers can necessarily profit from a par-
ticular curriculum, the course of study, except for certain minimal
requirements, will be adjusted to suit individual needs and inter-
ests."[7] The only course required of all students is the workshop in
which only student work is read and criticized. Whether intended or
not, the effect of this curriculum is to isolate the beginning poet from
the literary past.

On the other hand, maybe this is unavoidable given the institu-
tional constraints even the best-intentioned writing programs face.
Unavoidable, and especially unfortunate now that it has fallen to the
writing programs to attempt to do some of the work once performed
by departments of English. As more and more scholars and critics
ignore or minimize the aesthetic dimensions of literature in favor of
the extra-aesthetic values and biases at work in literary texts, more
and more writers are called on to impart a sensitivity to literary style.
But whereas the traditional Ph.D. program entails several years of
intensive study, the MFA program is only two years long. And since
those two years provide, for most students, the only opportunity
they'll ever have to devote themselves entirely to their writing, they
naturally shy away from academic work. Even those who don't avoid
academic courses have time only to sample the great poetry of the
past. They simply are not given the opportunity to study literature in
enough detail to acquire a historically informed sensitivity to literary
works. For the most part, the message implicit in the length and struc-
ture of our programs is that the repertoire of forms, conventions, and
technical strategies which the poets in previous periods utilized for
the investigation of human experience are either irrelevant to the stu-
dent's "individual needs and interests," or so many impediments to
the realization of his or her distinctive sensibility or voice.[8]

3

Of the poets Dante meets in Limbo, Horace would have been the one
who has the most to say about the education of the poet, for his best
known poem, the verse epistle to the Piso family, later titled by Quin-

tilian, "Art of Poetry," served for generations of later writers as a creative writing handbook, perhaps the first of its kind. Though informal and loosely organized in keeping with the conventions of the letter poem, "Art of Poetry" describes in detail the sort of education Horace believes all poets need; it exemplifies the integrative vision of what poetry and the poet ought to be, bringing together qualities we now too comfortably assume are found only in separation.

There is no controversy or debate for Horace over whether poetic excellence is the result of "nature or conscious art," whether poets are born or made. Study and native ability, training and talent, are equally important. Poets can and must be educated and trained. But training, in turn, presupposes genius in need of cultivation: "For my part, I do not see the value of study without native ability, nor of genius without training: so completely does each depend on the other and blend with it."[9] Even the most naturally gifted student requires years of professional study, or as Sidney following Horace would later write, just "as the fertilest ground must be manured, so must the high flying wit have a Daedalus to guide him."[10] Thus Horace reserves his most scathing satire for both the mad poet who believes that "native genius is better than wretched art," and the supercilious amateur who likewise dares "to write poetry without knowing how to do it. 'Why not?' he thinks. He is a free man, well-born, perhaps with a knight's income, and has a good character." The true poet, on the other hand, possesses intimate knowledge of every aspect of his art: "If I am unable to understand and retain these clear-cut distinctions and poetic genres, why would I be considered a poet? Why, through false shame, should I prefer to be ignorant rather than to know?"[11]

Learning implies instruction. And at the heart of classical instruction lay the doctrine of imitation. Yet here too as Horace describes it imitation combines the contrary values of originality and adherence to a model. The "well-instructed imitator" doesn't produce museum pieces or mechanical copies; he doesn't "translate word for word, nor jump into a narrow imitative groove, from which both fear and the rules followed in the given work prevent [his] escape."[12] Rather he develops his distinctive powers of imagination by adapting what he imitates to suit his own experience.

The doctrine of imitation challenges certain deeply held contemporary notions about the self and the creative process. First, it assumes that one writes not necessarily to uncover a self already fully formed and waiting to be found, but to imagine oneself as otherwise than as one is. Authenticity or self-acceptance is less the aim of this sort of writing than inclusiveness. And this, in turn, implies that each specific mode of being, like poetry itself, can be revised over time to accommodate previously excluded or unencountered ranges of experience. One's voice, in other words, isn't fixed or fated, but mutable, something continuously made and remade out of other voices.

Second, the creative process this entails is paradoxically cooler and more rapturous than it appears in our standard accounts. Insofar as imitation is an exercise of conscious will, it contradicts our feeling that artistic excellence ultimately derives from inspiration. Yet insofar as it suggests and encourages the taking over of one voice by another, it involves, as well, a kind of mystical possession. Longinus, for instance, regards imitation as a kind of metempsychosis whereby "from the natures of the great men of old there are borne in upon the souls of those who emulate them what we may describe as effulgences, so that even those who seem little likely to be possessed are thereby inspired and succumb to the spell of the others' greatness."[13] Likewise, for Ben Jonson, the well-instructed imitator fosters his individual talent by converting "the substance, or riches of another poet, to his own use." He doesn't swallow what he takes in, "crude, raw, or indigested," but "feedes with an appetite and hath a stomache to concoct, devide, and turne all into nourishment."[14] One chooses the food one eats but the process by which that food is turned to nourishment transcends the will. In the work of Ezra Pound, the modern poet perhaps most interested in imitation, will and rapture are sometimes so difficult to tell apart that one often comes disguised as the other. Early in his career he affected an air of Dionysian mystery in his imitations of the troubadour poets of twelfth-century Provençal, claiming that his own voice had been taken over wholly by the voice of those earlier writers. Yet the poems seem now, in retrospect, more rhetorically overblown than mystical, more staged than rapt. On the other hand, toward the end of his career when he was incarcerated at St. Elizabeth's and literally surrounded by the demonically possessed, he chose to imitate or loosely translate the odes of Confucius, poems devoted not to Dionysian transport but to the celebration of civic order, public health, and social being. Yet these poems are much more convincing recreations and adaptations of a foreign voice, more genuinely mystical for all their surface coolness.

Third, imitation challenges our concept of originality. For the writers in this tradition originality has little to do with producing work that bears no trace of past achievement, with making something up ex nihilo, out of whole cloth. Idiosyncrasy—the peculiar and unique (idio) conjunction or synthesis of disparate materials, conventions, or styles—better describes their view. Imagination is the crucible in which external literary and extraliterary influences gather and combine in new and distinctive ways with internal need, disposition, temperament. The more and better influences one can draw on, then, the better chance there'll be for original expression. Thus, according to David Armstrong, what makes the odes of Horace so unique is the application of thirteen Greek lyric meters (most of which were entirely new to Latin) "to a vocabulary as different as possible from that of the Greek poets Horace imitates, a purposely limited and purist vocabulary almost without compound adjectives, Greek words, or dialect and popular Latin usages."[15]

In this light the ancient quarrel over whether poetic excellence is the result of native talent or learning, originality or tradition, is really just a quarrel over emphasis. This is why the same writers who side with originality or nature often show a powerful though tacit commitment, in practice if not in theory, to the opposing value. So Pindar in the second "Olympian Ode" can praise the originality of the poet "who knows many things by nature," and denigrate the poets whom he calls "mere learners." Yet in the gnomic and encomiastic sections of his work, as Bruno Gentili points out, Pindar closely adheres to the canons of "genre" composition and so acknowledges his debt to tradition.[16] Likewise in restoration England, Dryden can say at one point in "An Essay on Dramatic Poesy" that Shakespeare was "naturally learned" and therefore required no specialized training, and at another point in the same essay that "those great men whom we propose to ourselves as patterns of our imitation, serve us as a torch, which is lifted up before us, to illumine our passage and often elevate our thoughts as high as the conception we have of our author's genius."[17] Samuel Johnson, too, a little later, opposing the too bookish, merely derivative verse of Gray, Warton, and their school, counseled poets to turn more generously to the world around them, arguing that "No man was ever yet great by imitation."[18] Yet his two greatest poems, "Vanity of Human Wishes" and "London," are imitations of Juvenal. Even in the romantic and modern periods when classical ideas of art and artistic education had fallen out of fashion, poets still learned to write by studying and imitating earlier poets: think of Keats in "Endymion" imitating Spenser's "The Faerie Queen," or

William Carlos Williams in "The Wanderer" imitating "Endymion."

One could argue that all beginning poets are witting or unwitting imitators, and that this is just as true for the young American poet today as it is for his or her counterpart in earlier generations. Well, yes and no. For insofar as our creative writing programs are unable to provide a firm grounding in the literary past, our poets are left with no one to imitate but their own contemporaries or their teachers. And this as much as anything accounts for the dreary sameness of so much contemporary verse—a colossal irony in light of our belief (implicit in the way we teach creative writing) that imitation inhibits "voice" and self-expression.

Again, even the romantics and moderns relied on imitation in their artistic maturity as well as in their youth. In adapting Miltonic blank verse to suit the needs of the interior epic of "The Prelude," Wordsworth is imitating in the free and creative way that Horace urges. So too is Stevens in adapting Wordsworthian blank verse to suit the postsymbolist, postromantic needs of "Sunday Morning." Williams is also imitating in the classical spirit in "To Elsie" or in any number of his flower poems in which he makes the pastoral tradition of European verse responsive to an industrial American landscape. His great poem, "The Descent," with its triadic, step-down line and its conception of memory as an underworld of shadows, is in effect an American reworking of Dante's terza rima and his Christian hell. As much for these poets as for Horace, imitation blends the critical and creative faculties. It does not slavishly reproduce the past; it rather brings the past and present into quarrelsome and loving dialogue. It joins us to the traditions we inherit and at the same time sharpens our perception of what's uniquely ours.

Finally, imitation can also provide a way of critically intervening in the social or literary scene. In imitating a forgotten or neglected poet or kind of poem, a poet can demonstrate what the prevailing fashions overlook or exclude, or what the culture threatens. At a time of cultural disintegration, Ezra Pound turned to the odes of Confucius. In the mid-seventies Robert Pinsky attempted to correct the hermetic imagistic bias of contemporary American poetry by imitating the discursive mode of the Horatian letter-poem in his book-length poem, *An Explanation of America*.

Which is to say, all of these poets would have eagerly joined the conversation there in Limbo and said things the other poets would have been interested to hear.

4

According to Horace, though, the aspiring poet requires more than extensive learning and the training, exercise, and expressive range that imitation provides. He or she also needs a mentor, someone who can "teach the duty and office of the poet, instruct him where to get his materials, show what moulds and develops him, what is fitting to him and what is not, where the good can lead him and where the wrong."[19] The true instructor doesn't merely "encourage." Nor does he only offer technical expertise. He also imparts a theoretical understanding of poetry itself; he draws out the aesthetic and extra-aesthetic consequences of the poems put before him, showing "where the good can lead him and where the wrong."

Is it possible to do this in a two-year program? Most of the students I have worked with in my fifteen years of teaching creative writing have been rightly obsessed with their own poetry. And much as I've tried to persuade them that they'll need to eavesdrop, sooner or later, on the conversation of the masters in order to enrich their own distinctive powers of expression; much as I've quoted Eliot "that not only the best, but the most individual parts [of a poet's work] may be those in which the dead poets, his ancestors, assert their immortality most vigourously," they have understandably preferred to devote what little time the writing program gives them—time they may never have again—to the poetry they feel they want to write. And much as I believe in the necessity of teaching "the duty and office of the poet," the better part of my pedagogical energies has been spent in workshops encouraging and facilitating "self-expression." The qualities expected of me and which I therefore have felt compelled to cultivate are generosity of taste, heightened receptivity, imaginative sympathy, the capacity to enter into any kind of work and appreciate it on its own terms, aesthetically, whether or not it is the kind of work I do myself. Like most workshop instructors, I struggle to divine within the most abused, disfigured poem the ideal poem the student is struggling to realize, and I try to make the technical suggestions that will help him or her realize it.

Under the current setup, maybe the most that any of us can be is the pedagogical equivalent of Keats' "chameleon poet," suppressing our own beliefs and values in favor of the technical problems posed by the poems set before us. And while I do not mean to disparage such an openness and flexibility of mind, what Keats calls "negative capabili-

ty," I can't help but feel along with W. S. Di Piero that as teachers
(and poets) we've grown a little too comfortable with our uncertain-
ties, mysteries, and doubts, and that we would better serve our stu-
dents if like Horace's ideal teacher we reached a little more irritably
after fact and reason.[20] The two-year workshop-oriented program has
made us very good at imparting an appreciation of certain microscop-
ic subtleties of language, but not so good at attending to the general
ideas and values implicit in each kind of poem or poetic style, ideas
and values about language and mind, self and world, which have
moral as well as artistic consequences.

Every way of writing presupposes an implicit judgment about
experience. Even the formal principles within a poem, which govern
the selection and arrangement of details, attitudes, and tones, are
implicitly evaluating what we should see and how we should see it,
highlighting some aspect of reality, some possibility of being, by dim-
ming others. Style in the broadest sense, encompassing everything
from rhythm to word choice, is consciousness in action, and we fail as
teachers if we do not make our students even question whether some
ways of writing allow a freer more energetic play of consciousness
than others. But to examine both the limitations and advantages
which a given style affords is to move beyond mere technical analysis;
at this level, aesthetic questions verge on moral ones. And it is just
such questions we find it difficult to raise.

There are many reasons for this (beyond the time constraints I've
already mentioned): our suspicion, as postmodern skeptics (which we
typically carry to a puritanical extreme), that *all* value judgments
outside the hard sciences are subjective and arbitrary assertions of
will or merely of veiled self-interest; our dislike, as American demo-
cratic egalitarians, of anything that smacks of hierarchy, a dislike
that's vital for political matters but disastrous for literary ones; and,
as a consequence of this, our peculiarly American faith in technology,
or how-to-ism, believing that everything, art included, is reducible to
a surefire technique to be neutrally imparted to our students (in the
poetry workshop the extreme focus on technique goes hand in hand
with an extremely mystifying technical language, one extreme perhaps
compensating for the other).

A good teacher should know how to talk in intimate detail about
any kind of poem. He should also encourage, and not be overly criti-
cal. "No more," Ben Jonson remarks, "would I tell a greene Writer all
his faults, lest I should make him grieve and faint, and at last

despaire. For nothing doth more hurt, then to make him so afraid of all things, as hee can endeavour nothing."[21] On the other hand, if encouragement is all a teacher offers, if he only tries to help the student write the poem he or she is interested in writing, without at the same time showing "what moulds and develops him, what is fitting to him and what is not fit"—that is, without at the same time helping students to discriminate among expressive possibilities—if the teacher fails to address or even raise the extra-aesthetic questions of the worth of this or that way of writing, he becomes, at best, an aesthetic technocrat, at worst an aesthetic therapist ("My poem's OK, your poem's OK").

5

Writing programs have come in for a good deal of criticism in the last few years. In prominent magazines and journals throughout the country, Donald Hall, Joseph Epstein, Greg Kuzma, Dana Gioia, Ted Solotaroff, and others have blamed creative writing for the decline of American poetry from an art with broad cultural appeal to a specialized activity confined to the closed world of the classroom.[22] Poetry, these critics tell us, is read only by other poets, all of whom either teach or study in the writing programs. The "common reader," the "nonspecialist intellectual," who comprises the "general culture" no longer turns to poetry for news about the world. That institutional pressures have shaped the practice of poetry since it moved into the university is undeniably true. The amazing amount of mediocre verse one sees in pamphlets, chapbooks, books, anthologies, journals, and magazines is partly a result of the unavoidable policy of admitting students to MFA programs not on the basis of talent but to keep enrollments up; and it's partly the result of poets who teach in these programs needing to publish early and often to advance up the academic ladder.

On the other hand, there has always been a lot of mediocre verse to go around, even before the writing programs came along. Take the 1912 edition of *The Lyric Year*, an annual anthology selected from one year's work of a hundred American poets. For the 1912 edition, the editor, Ferdinand Earle, who would later marry Charlotte Herman, sister of William Carlos Williams' wife, Florence, received over "ten thousand poems by nearly two thousand writers of verse." Williams himself was among the two thousand poets who entered the competition. He was also among the one thousand nine hundred who didn't win. Given how much larger our population is today than in 1912, is there really that much more bad verse being written? Is it really any harder now for good work to find an audience? Williams himself was in his late fifties before anyone outside a small circle of fellow artists read his work.[23]

In any event, to claim that writing programs are responsible for the formation of what Gioia calls a university-supported poetry subculture insulated from a general audience is to mistake effects for causes. It may tell us something about why no one outside the university is reading contemporary poetry, but it tells us nothing about why no one outside the university is reading poetry at all. The so-called general reader that Gioia, Epstein, and Solotaroff invoke isn't just ignoring the poetry our writing programs are producing; he or she is ignoring poetry altogether, Tennyson as much as Tillinghast, Horace as much as Heaney. No one is curling up in bed at night with Palgrave's *Golden Treasury*.

Poetry is, for good or ill, a highly specialized use of language, and the news it offers requires, beyond intelligence and sensitivity, a good deal of concentrated effort, patience, and time, qualities our frenetic, hyperspecialized culture keeps in short supply. The educated reader is most likely a professional who can barely keep up with the advances in his own field, much less delve into others in the little spare time he has. His or her need for news about the way we live now is more easily satisfied by the much less demanding media of film, television, and the press. In pointing this out, I am not making a nostalgic appeal to the good old days before mass media came to dominate how we spent our leisure time. It's important, though, to keep in mind the profound effects mass media have had on the way we satisfy our appetite for knowledge, and the way this in turn has affected our interest in the arts. For instance, it was not unusual in East Germany before the fall of communism for a book of poems by a relatively unknown poet to sell over ten thousand copies. In a society where information was carefully controlled, people turned to poetry and fiction to learn whatever they could about the world. When the socialist government fell, however, and information was more freely available in newspapers, magazines, and other media, the sale of poetry collections fell dramatically. As Samuel Johnson once remarked, "People in general do not willingly read, if they can have anything else to amuse them."[24]

In America, the common reader, at least as Johnson understood him, is now the professional student of literature. And those outside the university who still read serious literature for pleasure and knowledge do so because they studied it in college. The common reader of serious literature, in other words, is, for the most part, either a specialist or has been trained by one.[25] Moreover, aside from college and professional sports, McDonalds, Pac-Man, and Teenage Mutant Ninja Turtles, our culture is itself composed of subcultures, a crazy quilt of specialized pursuits, enclaves, coteries—all existing in isolation from each other. The so called "general culture" that the critics of creative writing claim our poetry no longer speaks to is an antiquated fiction. As James Clifford observes,

> In a world with too many voices speaking all at once, a world where syncretism and parodic invention are becoming the rule, not the exception, an urban, multinational world of institutional transience—where American clothes made in Korea are worn by young people in Russia, where everyone's roots are in some degree cut—in such a world it becomes increasingly difficult to attach human identity and meaning to a coherent culture or language.[26]

Or, for that matter, to posit the existence of a common reader. That poetry no longer reaches such an illusory creature is a moot point.

6

Poetry can be taught, if one has the talent to learn it. The health of the art itself depends on how well it's taught. Poets have always needed training, and teachers to train them. They have always sought out the conversation of other poets, of older poets, of those who have mastered what the younger poet is setting out to learn. Certainly there are writers who have gotten all they needed from reading and writing on their own, but the autodidact is the exception, not the rule. And for every autodidact there are many equally talented poets who for want of proper training might never realize their gifts.

But if creative writing is to be genuinely educative and not merely, as it often seems, either a poor man's group therapy or a makeshift preparation for careers in teaching, we will need to rethink how and why we teach the way we do. We need to reexamine some of the quasi-romantic notions that currently inform the workshops. We need, I think, to reacquaint ourselves with what the classical tradition has to say about the education of the poet. This does not mean going back to that tradition and following the letter of everything it recommends; rather it means adapting it to suit our present needs and interests, which is to say, to imitate it in a classical spirit, freely and creatively.

Even the most thorough program is no guarantee that everyone who passes through it will become a poet. Becoming a poet, as Horace reminds us, involves more than technical mastery; it involves native ability and inspiration, neither of which is reducible to techniques one can talk about or impart. And one can finally only teach what one can talk about. The Piso brothers could not have had a better teacher than Horace, or been given better advice than what he tells them in the "Art of Poetry." Yet where are they today?

If we were to reform our writing programs along Horatian lines, we would first of all redesign the curriculum so as to integrate literary study and creative writing.

This is an especially good moment to attempt such a reformation. As I mentioned earlier, the intense attention to literary style which literary study emphasizes and which imitation exercises help refine is no longer widespread in English departments. It's not that English professors are no longer teaching literature, but rather that their interests have shifted from literature as aesthetic artifact with its own internal laws and conventions to literature as cultural artifact whose aesthetic features often mask political, racial, and sexual biases. What professors of literature now seek to develop in themselves and in their students is skepticism and distrust. This is, in my view, an entirely laudable aim. The "hermeneutics of suspicion" has greatly enriched our understanding of the ways in which literary practices participate in cultural history. It has helped us reexamine and revise the values that underlie our literary judgments, and made us more hospitable to the work of people who till recently were either misrepresented in the books we taught, or not represented at all. But skeptical detachment is not the only attitude to bring to literary works. A full and intimate understanding of literature also requires, initially at least, emotional and intellectual attachment, possession, identification, an active yielding or opening of the self to unfamiliar possibilities of being, if only to gain a keener feeling for whatever human biases those possibilities consciously or unconsciously promote. It requires first and foremost the sympathetic imagination that enables us to enter into a poem or story, however foreign to our taste or values, and appreciate it from the inside, as it were, so as to experience how its meaning, its stance toward life, is interwoven into every aspect of its style. When applied to literature, a "hermeneutics of suspicion," in and of itself, despite its intellectual sophistication, is as crudely incomplete as a sympathetic imagination divorced from the disciplines of intellectual and historical inquiry. Both habits of mind ought to sustain and nourish one another. In any event, by integrating literary study and creative writing through the practice of imitation, we would not only provide our students with a better education; we would also help preserve a historically informed sensitivity to style, a sensitivity which otherwise may atrophy in the current intellectual climate.

To effect such a reformation we would have to lengthen the course of study from two to five years, at the very least, so that students would have a genuine opportunity to study great literature in intimate detail, not merely sample it. I realize that a longer and more rigorous program will seem impractical from an institutional viewpoint (administrators, like cattle ranchers, prefer programs that herd the largest numbers in and out as quickly as possible); and it will also seem impractical from the viewpoint of the would-be poetry professionals (students for whom graduate study is merely a career move toward a job as a professional teacher of creative writing). What a longer program would foster is not the premature professionalism so endemic to the present system, but a view of and respect for poetry as a learned profession which requires of its students an impractical, unprofessional patience and dedication.

The assumption governing both the seminar and the workshop would be that a knowledge of the history of an art is indispensable to the practice of the art. Moreover, in keeping with the Horatian integrative spirit, students would be required to work in more than a single genre, instead of specializing prematurely as they do now. In addition to broadening their repertoire of expressive possibilities, students in different genres would have more opportunity to interact and learn from each other. As they are currently organized, our MFA programs not only ghettoize the creative writers from the scholars and critics, they also ghettoize the poets and fiction writers from each other, to the detriment of both. With more training in the art of fiction, the poet would acquire a greater feel for telling stories, for narrative structure and depiction of character—which might enable him or her to regain some of the experiential territory lost over the years to prose. Likewise, with more training in the art of poetry, the novelist or short story writer would be able to draw on a wider range of rhythmical, imagistic, and figurative resources.

Finally, throughout the five years of the program, there would be as many imitations and translations as "original" compositions in the workshops. Students would read an assigned text, say, Dante's *Inferno*, and write imitations of it over the course of the semester. The achievements of the past, not merely their own experience, would provide the fuel of their development, and their development, in turn, would lead not to their own voice speaking in isolation but to their voice in conversation with the poets who've preceded them, and from whom they have inherited the very art they speak with now.

1991

Notes

1   Dante, *Inferno*, trans. Charles Singleton (Princeton, 1980), 41.

2.   Ibid.

3.   Robert Graves, *The White Goddess: A Historical Grammar Of Poetic Myth* (New York, 1972), 23, 457.

4.   *AWP Catalogue of Writing Programs*, 3d ed. (Norfolk, 1980), 55 (hereafter referred to as *AWP*).

5.   Marvin Bell, *Old Snow Melting* (Ann Arbor, 1983), 104.

6.   *Finding The Words: Conversations With Writers Who Teach*, ed. Bunge (Athens, 1985), 66.

7.   *AWP*, 108.

8.   I want to thank David Meyers, an ex-graduate student at Northwestern University who in 1987 referred me both to *Old Snow Melting* and to *Finding The Words*, as well as to the *AWP* quotations.

9.   Horace, "Art of Poetry," in *Criticism: The Major Texts*, ed. W.J. Bate (New York, 1970), 57.

10. Sir Philip Sidney, "An Apology For Poetry," in *Criticism: The Major Texts*, 101.

11. Horace, "Art Of Poetry," 52.

12. Ibid., 53.

13. Longinus, "On The Sublime," in *Criticism: The Major Texts*, 68.

14. Ben Jonson, "Timber: Or, Discoveries," in *Criticism: The Major Texts*, 115.

15. David Armstrong, *Horace* (New Haven, 1989), 69.

16. Bruno Gentili, *Poetry and Its Public in Ancient Greece*, trans. A. Thomas Cole (Baltimore, 1988), 53.

17. John Dryden, "An Essay Of Dramatic Poesy," in *Criticism: The Major Texts*, 149.

18. Samuel Johnson, *Rasselas*, in *Criticism: The Major Texts*, 206.

19. Horace, "Art of Poetry," 56.

20. See W. S. Di Piero, *Memory and Enthusiasm* (Princeton, 1989), 73: "Keats' remark about Negative Capability seems to be becoming a literary cult object. The commentators are full of it these days. Some, though, use it as a justification of ignorance. Embrace doubt and uncertainty, the current wisdom has it, for it will do you good. Indeed, it will ennoble you. I suppose it's easy to heroize one's fearlessness in the presence of uncertainty. We travesty Keats' inquiring, sensuous intelligence, however, if we cite him as an endorsement of the unwillingness to pass judgment, to evaluate, to assert or deny. Negative Capability is no counsel for failed nerve. Keats was advising himself to be patient in the quest for definitiveness. It is the counsel of patience of the imagination."

21. Ben Jonson, "Timber: Or, Discoveries," 113.

22. See Donald Hall, "Poetry and Ambition," *Kenyon Review* (Fall 1983); Greg Kuzma, "The Catastrophe of Creative Writing," *Poetry* 148 (1986); Joseph Epstein, "Who Killed Poetry?" *Commentary* 86, no. 2 (August 1988); Ted Solotaroff, "The Literary Campus and the Person of Letters," in *A Few Good Voices In My Head* (New York, 1987), 241-56; Dana Gioia, "Can Poetry Matter?" *Atlantic Monthly* 267, no. 5 (May 1991).

23. See *The Collected Poems of William Carlos Williams*, vol. 1: 1909–39, ed. Litz & MacGowan (New York, 1986), 477.

24. *Boswell's Life of Johnson*, ed. G. B. Hill and L. F. Powell (Oxford, 1964), iv, 218 (May 1, 1783).

25. For a trenchant discussion of the fallacy of the common reader see Frank Kermode, "The Common Reader," in *An Appetite For Poetry* (Cambridge, 1989), 95.

26. James Clifford, *The Predicament of Culture* (Cambridge, 1988), 95.

The Early Seventies and J. V. Cunningham

As I sat before him in his verse writing class in 1970, J. V. Cunningham seemed an odd mix of frailty and resilience. White hair combed back from his craggy forehead, stoop-shouldered and coughing now and again from the Camels he chainsmoked in and out of class, he seemed much older than his 59 years. Yet his direct gaze when he would talk to you, and his sharp wit that would not suffer fools or foolish writing gladly, made him a daunting figure. He sat informally on a table at the front of the room, with one leg crossed or rather wrapped around the other, as he read out the student poem we, the twenty or so class members, would have to criticize. He never told us who wrote the student poems we discussed, though this time everybody knew that it was mine because I sat there as casual as a sphinx, sweating and blushing from the desperate effort to seem unconcerned. This was the first poem I had turned in to the class. I can't recall anything about it except that it was written, like most of my poems then, in an Olsonesque free verse, what Cunningham called "lineated prose." I should say that Cunningham never made copies of student poetry. He read each poem out and expected us to talk about it having heard it only once. This, he said, would train our powers of retention. Whatever in the poem was memorable we would retain. And what wasn't memorable wasn't worth writing in the first place. Well, obviously the class felt there was nothing memorable in my poem for they said nothing when he finished reading it. After an interminable silence in which I contemplated some alternative career, Cunningham held my poem up and said in a voice that emphysema lowered to a whisper, "This is nothing more than spilled ink," and proceeded to the next poem.

I was a typical Brandeis undergraduate writer. What literary training I had had extended back no farther than the Beat poets, the Black Mountain school, and rock music. Ginsberg, Ferlinghetti, Creeley, and Dylan were my cultural heroes. I was one of the "ambitious boys" Cunningham defines himself against in "For My Contemporaries," someone for whom poetry was a spiritual calling, trafficking in feelings which I believed were more poetic the more ineffable they were. Moreover, these were such highly politicized times that questions of literary form became questions of political affiliation. In so much of the poetry and criticism I admired formality came under a kind of psychopolitical attack in which form and technique in general became synonymous with rationality and repression, and free verse with liberated feeling and imagination. As Paul Breslin has noted, politics came to be regarded as psychology writ large, and psychology in turn as politics internalized. Hence what technology—the product of a hyperrational culture—was doing to the North Vietnamese, our hypermetrical technique was doing to our own emotions.

Yet here I was, faced with a man for whom poetry was a definitive statement, in meter, of something worth saying, for whom thinking and feeling, intellectual exactitude of statement and emotional precision, were not exclusive possibilities. Meter, he told us, was the ground bass of poetry; regularity was the last variation; and the contemporary literary scene, which I revered, he believed was in a woeful mess. There was too wide a diversity of metrical forms and systems available to the beginning poet, and too much phonetic ignorance. The triumph of the New Criticism had turned reading poetry into a demonstration of interpretive finesse, the more elaborate the better. And our rebellious attitude, which we inherited, whether we knew it or not, from our Modernist forebears, was sufficient to destroy the old tradition, but not to establish a new one in its place. He was a wry, epigrammatic Jeremiah whose teaching method, like the method of his scholarship and poetry, was definitive, aphoristic, brief. Just as in his poems he often strips away the details and circumstances of experience, leaving the reader with an abstract statement or definition, so in his writing class he would declare, "This doesn't work," "there's too much of the pretty-pretty here," "the meter falls flat on its face," and so on, and leave it up to us to figure out why this was so.

Without explanation, he told us that all good poetry has a quality of "just rightness" about it. And when we pressed him to elaborate he would recite Frost's "Acquainted with the Night," or Stevens' "The House was Quiet and the World was Calm" and then remark that after reading such a poem all you want to do is smoke a cigarette and contemplate. "Just rightness" was something you either recognized or didn't. Like a good joke, it was what did not require explanation. If we didn't see it now, through study and experience we'd see it later. All of us, though, understood the concept negatively by the end of the semester—it was everything our poems weren't. Late in that freshman year, I brought him what I was certain was my best poem. He read it through and said, "Mr. Shapiro, if I liked that sort of thing, I'd say you did it very well." That would have to do for praise.

If such a tight-lipped pedagogical style puzzled, vexed and sometimes pained us, it also proved to be enormously inspiring. Those of us who stuck with his class never mistook his pointed judgments for contempt or condescension. We understood that he was giving us, unfailingly, the respect of serious attention. Poetry is an exacting discipline. In refusing to flatter our desire to be poets, Cunningham instilled in us a sense of how difficult it is to write well and unforgettably. He never expected or wanted us to write like him or think like him. His reticence was partly a safeguard against unduly influencing us. He never wanted disciples or epigones. He wanted us to entertain the questions he was raising, and to challenge our inherited assumptions and pieties as rigorously as he had challenged his. He had the long view of the literary past. We had the short view. He felt it was his responsibility as a teacher and older poet to show us that in correcting the excesses of our New Critical fathers, setting our immediacy and informality against their Olympian tension and sophisticated wit, we were only repeating the excesses of our Modernist grandfathers. As a friend of mine is fond of saying, what to us had seemed Hegelian dialectic, to Cunningham was Empedoclean flux.

Despite his wariness about influencing students, I sometimes wonder if the polarized thinking, which the highly charged political climate of the times had generated, didn't exaggerate his temperamental reticence, making him more remote, more unapproachable than he otherwise might have been. He never attempted to befriend us. He never lingered after class for conversation. When the bell rang he bolted. His private conferences were likewise brisk and businesslike. On the other hand, given our differences of age and experience, why should he have befriended us? How could we have been anything to him but students? We were East Coast baby-boomers, children of middle- and upper-middle-class affluence. Our revolutionary zeal was predicated on material well-being. We could imagine Utopian fulfillment because most of our material needs had never gone unmet. Cunningham was a Westerner, a child of the Depression. Years later, in response to an essay I had written on his work, an essay in which I say that the vision of experience implicit in so many of his poems is one of penury and want, he wrote me, saying as a personal note that "Black Tuesday, though not alluded to in any poem, was the basic experience of my life." He was at the time a runner in the dominant brokerage house in Denver; after the market crashed, he and his brother drifted through the West, doing free-lance writing for trade journals and living an uncertain, hand-to-mouth existence. The institutions we took for granted, or wanted to abolish, to Cunningham were precarious and frail. Personal experience had conditioned him to think that things, bad as they were, could get a good deal worse if they were trifled with. This feeling bordered on a quietistic resignation, and resignation seemed then, and still seems now, an inappropriate response to Vietnam.

That he respected us, and elicited respect from us, across the distance these differences created is a tribute to what I now see as his warmth and generosity, however aloof and unapproachable he appeared to me back then. A year or so after I had graduated, I was living in Ireland. I sent him some new poems and apologized for writing, assuming he'd regard it as an imposition. I was surprised, to say the least, when he wrote back saying, "Don't apologize for writing. I'm glad to hear from you, at any time, as often as you like." From that time on, until his death, we corresponded regularly, though it was only in the last five years of his life that we addressed each other by our first names. In my last note from him he congratulated me on my recent marriage: "It will be a new and fuller life—may it be a long one for both of you. So with customary and feeble words at a distance one signals his concern."

What I learned from Jim Cunningham's classes and later from his friendship, and what I continue to learn from his essays and poems, is that formality and feeling are both essential to our attentions to each other. Just as, in poetry, formal conventions of one kind or another mediate between private impulse and public utterance, self and other, so in life they enable us to make our individual experience accessible to someone else's understanding and sympathy. In this sense, formality is a kind of courtesy of attentiveness, a partial revelation and partial withholding of self so as to signal our concern, at a distance, in an act of generous and mutual respect.

1985